The Compleat
Muzzleloader

L. Gordon Stetser Jr.

Mountain Press Publishing Company
Missoula, Montana
1992

Illustrations by Trudi Peek

Library of Congress Cataloging-in-Publication Data

Stetser, L. Gordon, 1941-
    The compleat muzzleloader   /   L. Gordon Stetser, Jr.
      p.   cm.
    Includes bibliographical references and index.
    ISBN 0-87842-283-8
    1. Muzzle-loading firearms.   2. Muzzleloader hunting.   I. Title.
TS536.6.M8S84   1992   92-14077
799.2 ' 13—dc20   CIP

MOUNTAIN PRESS PUBLISHING COMPANY
2016 Strand Avenue • P.O. Box 2399
Missoula, Montana 59806
(406) 728-1900

For my family—

Dotti, Bob, Chris and Rick
for making the dreams come true.

Gordon

Table of Contents

Part III: Hunting With Muzzleloaders

—Robert K. Callahan

About the Author

L. Gordon Stetser Jr. is a freelance writer who has written many articles about muzzleloading guns, mountain men, the Civil War, bowhunting, and Americana and senior citizens' health topics.

His articles have appeared in such publications as Gun World, America's Civil War, American Hunter, Backwoodsman, Mature Living, Dakota Outdoors, Lady's Circle, Senior Life, and Mountain States Collector, and his columns are a regular feature of *Dakota Outdoors.*

The Compleat Muzzleloader is Gordon Stetser's first book. In it, he blends the historical uses of muzzleloading guns in North America with detailed how-to instructions. Although he wrote this book specifically for beginning shooters, it has much that will interest veterans of the sport as well.

Arms: That which makes men equal; a citizen's musket fires as well as a nobleman's.
—Heinrich Heine

PROLOGUE

Brown Bess

It was hot. The early morning sun beat down on the bone-weary American forces as they feverishly worked to fortify Breed's Hill above the Charles River near Bunker Hill. All through the night they had dug trenches. The morning light found them building up fence rows, piling hay, strengthening all the defenses they had put together in the darkness. They had been under fire from Redcoat artillery. The assault was hard for the untried colonial troops to weather, but they kept working throughout, unbroken.

Now it was time. The enemy began moving to the attack—2,300 British soldiers, lines perfectly straight, shoulder to shoulder. Nothing slowed them down. Line companies, light infantry, grenadiers, and marines, all in perfect formation. They were the best in the world, no one could deny it. One hundred feet away—the Americans should have broken ranks and run, but no one flinched. Fifty feet closer, and the colonists stood their ground, maybe too scared to move, or maybe just too impressed with what they saw.

Then it happened! No, the Americans didn't run. They opened fire. Everything in the trench exploded in a sheet of flame and lead ball. They waited until they'd seen the whites of the Redcoats' eyes. They aimed low. Their volley of buckshot and lead ball tore large holes in the perfect British lines. Each hit dropped another soldier. Those spared looked dazed as their comrades fell all around them.

The British tried three times to take that hill, but the volleys were too deadly. Then, ammunition gone, the Americans had to retreat. But by the time they withdrew, they had killed or wounded 1,054 of the British, almost half of the attacking force.

The Americans lost the Battle of Bunker Hill, but the British wanted no more victories at such cost.

The guns that inflicted the damage at Bunker Hill and in other battles of the Revolutionary War were not secret weapons; they were the standard muskets of the day. Whether American, British, French, or German in origin, all the muskets were remarkably alike. They were flintlocks with smooth bores, traits common since the reign of England's Queen Elizabeth I two centuries earlier. In her honor, and for the brown finish applied to the barrels, the English and early Americans affectionately called their muskets Brown Bess. Most measured from fifty-four to more than sixty inches in length and weighed twelve to fourteen pounds. Calibers ranged from .69 for French makes through .75 for British guns to a little more than .80 for some German models. At the beginning of the war, the Americans followed the British patterns, but after their alliance with

1

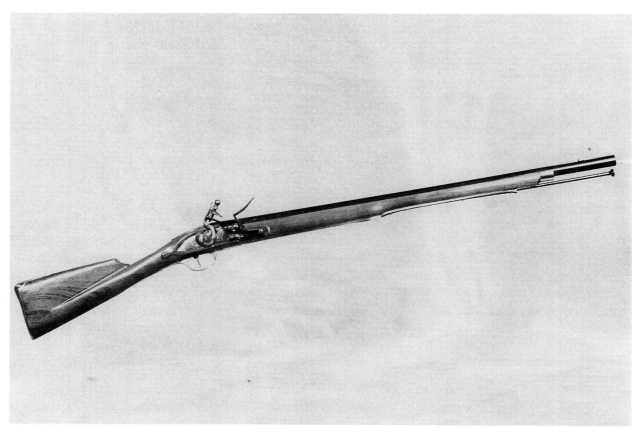

Brown Bess, a .75-caliber smoothbore musket. —Dixie Gun Works

France in 1777, they began imitating the French models.

The chief characteristic of all these muskets was their large, unrifled bores. The big balls of lead they shot had tremendous stopping power. Modern pointed bullets of smaller diameter and higher velocity can pass through fleshy tissue with relatively little concussion; but a ball three-quarters of an inch in diameter will almost always knock a person to the ground, no matter where it hits the body. Large bores, therefore, were an important factor in breaking up an attack such as that on Bunker Hill. In addition to a large single ball, troops often used three or four quarter-inch buckshot, adding more missiles and increasing their chances of a hit.

Unrifled barrels allowed the muskets to be loaded quickly. Soldiers with rifles had to make sure each ball fit tightly by centering it in a patch of greased linen and forcing it down the barrel, which took precious time. Each man shooting a smoothbore, however, simply dropped a loose-fitting ball down the barrel, cursorily tamped it with his ramrod, and fired. Some prepared paper cartridges ahead of time by wrapping a ball and a measured charge of powder together, ready for nearly instant use. To load, the soldier pulled a cartridge from his bag, bit off the paper end, poured a little powder into the flash pan, then dumped the remaining powder and ball down the barrel; the paper remnant served as a wad, and a quick plunge with the ramrod seated the works firmly, but no real force was used in the process.

Using such cartridges, a well-trained soldier could load and fire with admirable speed. In most European armies, a recruit had to fire fifteen shots within three minutes forty-five seconds—a sustained rate of fire of one shot every fifteen seconds—before he was excused from the "awkward squad." Astounding as this may seem when one

2

considers all the motions involved, modern shooters can match this speed with relatively little practice.

In accuracy, however, the musket left much to be desired. Since the ball fitted loosely, when fired it might leave the barrel at one slight angle or another, often sending the lead well away from its target. Major George Hanger, an expert Redcoat marksman quoted in the 1975 book, *The Founding City,* published by the *Philadelphia Inquirer,* had this to say about the standard muskets of his day:

> A soldier's musket, if not exceedingly ill-bored [as many of them were], will strike the figure of a man at eighty yards; it may even at 100, but a soldier must be very unfortunate indeed who shall be wounded by a common musket at 150 yards, provided his antagonist aims at him; and as to firing at a man 200 yards away with a common musket, you may just as well fire at the moon and have hopes of hitting your object. I do maintain and will prove, whenever called on, that no man was ever killed at 200 yards, by a common soldiers musket, by the person who aimed at him.

Eighteenth-century troopers worried little about accuracy. Most battles, like the one at Bunker Hill, took place between ranks in close formation. Soldiers fired shots in volleys on command. Individual targets mattered little, since conventional military configurations in those days grouped troops together in fairly tight masses. It was more important to fire as many bullets as possible in the general direction of the enemy, confident that a good percentage of the missles would inflict harm. The same theory applies today with automatic weapons that create fields of fire through which an enemy must pass. Muskets fired in volleys proved deadly during the Revolutionary War. Rifles—an excellent arm in the hands of a skilled marksman—were used mainly for scouting, sniping, and situations where accuracy counted. But the musket, with its four crashing bullets a minute and its vicious bayonet thrust if necessary, was the standard weapon for soldiers.

Part 1
Muzzleloaders of the Past

Chapter 1

Muskets and Rifles for a New Land

The All-American Rifle

"The most lethal widow and orphan maker in the world. . . . A superb arm. . . . Deadly at unheard of distances." These and similar comments are what people throughout the Western world said about the American rifle, the first truly American firearm.

The principle responsible for this "superb arm" came from Europe, where rifles had been made since 1500. The theory of rifling was widely understood. For reliable performance, the ball needed to fit the barrel tightly; The shooter either had to force a very slightly oversized ball down the barrel with heavy blows of his ramrod aided by hammerlike strokes from the powder flask, or he wrapped the smaller ball in a greased patch of linen or leather. Both methods are described in books written before 1650. Rifle shooting, once a popular sport in continental Europe, had largely died out except among professional gamekeepers and foresters by the time German, Swiss, and Dutch settlers reached Pennsylvania.

Germanic colonists first brought the rifle to America. They arrived in increasing numbers after 1710 and brought short, large-caliber rifles from their native lands. Some of the newcomers were gunsmiths who made more of these rifles in their new home. Although these were good weapons—highly accurate at short and medium ranges—the requirements of life on the frontier

soon dictated modifications that perfected the arms in both function and beauty.

Rifles in the new land needed to be accurate at long range, economical in operation, and easy to handle in wooded country. To improve accuracy New World gunsmiths lengthened the barrel, which also ensured the powder charge would burn completely. To conserve lead and powder, usually in short supply along the frontier, they decreased the bore size. While European rifles frequently had bores of .65 to .70 caliber, by the time of the Revolution American rifles averaged .45 to .60; and by the end of the century some went as small as .40. Smaller calibers yielded more bullets per pound of lead. They also reduced the amount of metal needed to fashion the barrel, thus decreasing the gun's weight and making it easier to handle. Stocks also grew lighter as the straight, thick butts gave way to a slender design with a graceful droop and a crescent-shaped butt plate that fitted the shooter's shoulder.

Other changes made the American rifles distinctive, too. New woods, especially curly maple, became popular. Brass or some other metal replaced the patch compartment covers in the stocks traditionally outfitted with a sliding piece of wood, bone, or horn. Some of the better specimens were adorned with typically American decorations carved into the wood, or inlaid in brass, pewter, or

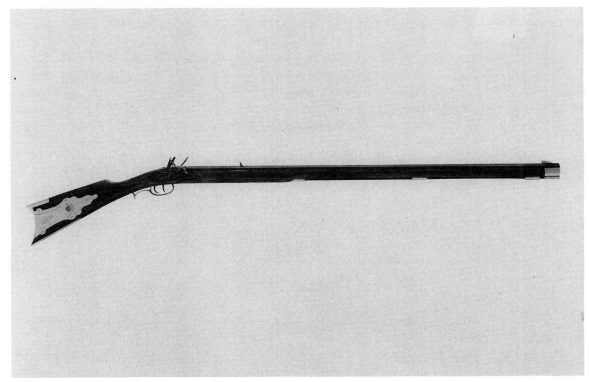

Pennsylvania Long Rifle. This .50-caliber flintlock owes it origins in the 1720s to the shorter German Jaeger hunting rifle. —Connecticut Valley Arms

silver along the stock. This is especially true after the Revolution. From 1785 to 1820 the arts of carving, inlaying, and engraving flourished.

The American rifle's evolution was slow, and it was not until around 1750 that it had changed enough to justify designating it as a new type. Some called it the Pennsylvania long rifle because that's where the first ones originated; others knew it as the Kentucky rifle because explorers and early settlers of that territory preferred it. By whichever name, the American rifle continued to develop in the grace of its design and decoration until about 1820. Thereafter, though it remained an accurate and efficient weapon, it deteriorated in appearance.

Much has been written about the American rifle's accuracy, and its performance was indeed amazing. When the first ten companies of Virginia and Maryland riflemen heeded the plea of Congress for soldiers and marched to Boston as the nucleus of the new American army, they delighted in demonstrating their skill to city folks unfamiliar with these new guns. One Virginian is said to have left the urbanites agog after putting eight consecutive shots through a five-by-seven-inch target at sixty yards. Indeed, it was considered no more than average shooting for a marksman to hit an enemy in the head at two hundred yards, or place a shot somewhere in his body at three to four hundred yards, if the wind wasn't too strong. No wonder the accuracy of the American rifle attracted worldwide attention.

The necessity of centering the ball in a patch before ramming it down the barrel made the American rifle slow to load compared to the smoothbore muskets. Because of this, and that it lacked a bayonet, the rifle's role in the Revolutionary War was restricted to special troops. Still, the rifle's accuracy made it an excellent weapon for light infantry and marksmen who served as snipers or

Kentucky Long Rifle. A .50-caliber weapon produced from the 1820s through the late 1850s. Many of the original flintlock ignitions were later converted to percussion cap styles. —Navy Arms

scouts. And for fighting the Indians along the frontier or dealing with the Indian allies of the British in the northern campaigns, it had no equal; but in the more formal warfare that characterized most of the conflict along the Atlantic seaboard, riflemen had to be backed up by regular infantry with their rapid-firing, four-shot-a-minute muskets and bayonets to keep the enemy from overrunning their positions.

The Battle of Kings Mountain in the Carolinas, where a group of frontier riflemen cornered and defeated a larger British force, stands out as a decided rifle victory during the Revolution. Also, in the War of 1812, rifles played a major role, along with artillery, to turn back a veteran British Army at the Battle of New Orleans. Sheltered by breastworks and supported by regular infantry, these riflemen used their arms to the best advantage, and the results were staggering: British casualties, 2,600; American, 13.

The American rifle became more than a superior weapon; it transcended its place in history and became part of the American legend.

The Plains Rifle

No one could call it beautiful. Its ancestors had been long, graceful rifles, light of bore, with fine carving and delicate inlays. This offspring had none of their grace. Its barrel was heavy, its bore large; its stock was thick and chunky with little decoration. But performance was its forte. It was designed for a special job and did it superbly. The men of the western mountains and plains had told gunsmiths exactly what they wanted in a gun; the result was the Plains rifle—or mountain rifle, as it was often called.

The famed Kentucky rifle developed earlier by the gunsmiths of Pennsylvania had served the frontiersmen of eastern America well. Relatively small game populated the wooded country east of the Mississippi River; except for moose in the north, deer and black bears were about the biggest animals one could expect to meet. Most men traveled on foot since they had little need to trek long distances, and the small caliber, long barrel, and light stock of the Kentucky rifle suited their needs perfectly.

But in the nineteenth century, as trappers and explorers spilled across the Mississippi into the newly acquired Louisiana Territory, their needs changed. They encountered vast, open country and longer distances to travel. Horses became the standard means of transportation; no one set out on foot if he could possibly avoid it. And larger game—bison, elk, and grizzly bears—required more powerful weapons. Small balls and light charges were worse than useless.

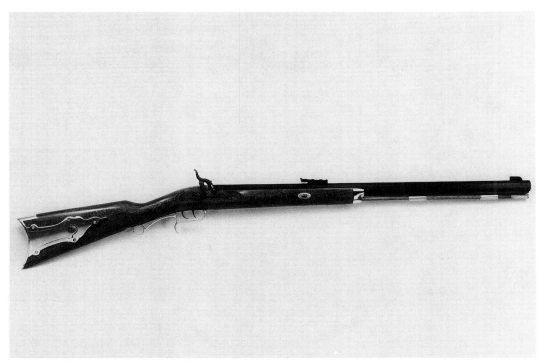

St. Louis Hawken. Many California-bound '49ers outfitted themselves with .50-caliber percussion rifles like this one . —Connecticut Valley Arms

Thus the rifle changed. The gunsmiths who moved from Pennsylvania into the Ohio River valley, and especially those who landed in St. Louis, made new rifles to meet the changing demands of their customers. Because long guns were a nuisance on horseback, they shortened the barrels to between twenty-eight and thirty-eight inches. They increased calibers from .45 to .55 for the larger game; and made the barrels heavy enough to handle a charge of powder equal in weight to the lead ball. They used sturdy stocks—sometimes running full length to the muzzle, sometimes halfway—that were thick in the wrist and wide in the butt. This design destroyed the gun's grace, but it created a stock that would not snap at the first fall from a horse's back. Though it was possible to decorate these guns, the plainsmen usually avoided any ornamentation that might glisten in the sunlight and either spoil their aim or attract an enemy's attention. In the harsh West, most preferred to put their money into features that would ensure performance rather than please the eye.

Other features also distinguished these firearms. They were heavy. Since the huge powder charges would have kicked unmercifully in a light arm, Plains rifles often weighed fifteen pounds or even a little more. The barrels were made of soft iron, and the rifling grooves spiraled gradually. Balls pushed by a hundred grains or more of powder would not always take rifling with a rapid twist—they might skip and fly wild unless charged exactly right—so the slow twist with soft iron permitted a wide variety of powder charges, even up to 215 grains, with no sacrifice of accuracy. Almost always the new rifles were percussion arms. Some early makes were flintlocks, but by the time the Plains rifle reached its full development, the older lock had become obsolete.

The Plains rifle was used by Jim Bridger, Kit Carson, Joe Meek, and their brethren on the Great Plains and in the Rockies. With it they slaughtered buffalo for food and fur, brought down mighty grizzlies, and fought the Sioux and Blackfeet. With its almost error-free reliability, its superb accuracy, and ability to shoot long range, it was a constant delight. Using such a rifle, Henry Chatillion astonished historian Frances Parkman by regularly dropping buffalo at three hundred yards or more with clean shots through their lungs.

Perhaps the best summary of the Plains rifle's capabilities, however, came many years after the weapon passed from common use, when a now-unknown marksman found a new specimen in St. Louis. Remembering with considerable skepti-

cism stories of its merit, he determined to give it a thorough test. He too, was astounded:

. . . I found that it would shoot straight with any powder charge up to a one-on-one load, equal weights of powder and ball. With a round ball of pure lead weighing 217 grains, patched with fine linen so that it fitted tight, and 205 grains of powder, it gave a very low trajectory and great smashing power, and yet the recoil was no more severe than that of a .45-caliber breechloader.

Although it was a fine arm for its day and purpose, conditions changed and gradually the Plains rifle faded from use, as its Kentucky forerunner had in an earlier time. The heyday of the fully developed percussion Plains rifle ran from 1820 through the late 1860s. The bigger, breechloading Sharps in particular became vastly popular and the slower muzzleloading rifles fell into disfavor.

These Thompson/Center Arms reproduction rifles imitate those carred across the western frontier by early pioneers.
—Thompson/Center

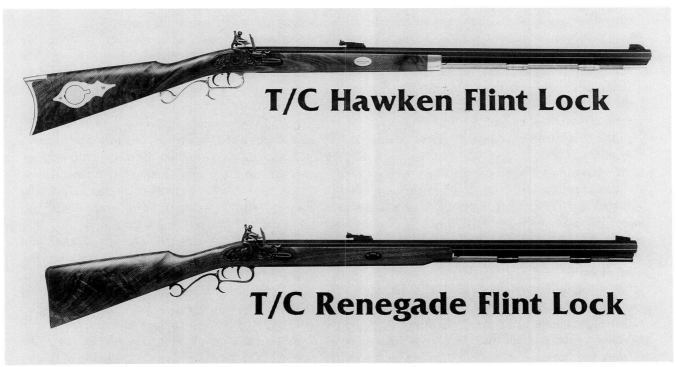

Chapter 2

The Civil War

Handguns of the Union Forces

In the spring of 1862 the beautiful valley between the Allegheny and Blue Ridge Mountains in northwest Virginia hummed with Confederate troops. Gen. Thomas "Stonewall" Jackson's famous Shenandoah Valley Campaign was getting under way. He sent Col. Turner Ashby and a cavalry contingent to scout the countryside for Yankees south of Harrisonburg. It was an easy search, and soon a group of blue-clad horseman rose to the bait. A textbook cavalry charge developed as opposing forces dashed at each other across an open field.

One of the Rebel leaders, Capt. Henry Gilmore, singled out a Union officer and galloped toward him, revolver in hand. As they closed, he fired twice, apparently without hitting his mark. The Union officer fired three or four shots and missed. Closer they came. Grimly, Gilmore saved his last shot until only a few feet separated the men. He could not miss at this range! The shot rang out, but still the Yankee kept coming. The Yankee's saber flashed, and the startled Gilmore summoned all his skill to avoid the swinging blade. Returning his empty revolver to his holster, he drew his own sword.

Boot-top to boot-top they fought in the classic cavalry tradition until the horseman in gray, whirling his saber, disarmed his adversary and took him prisoner. He then discovered why his bullets did not topple the Yankee. The blue coat covered a steel vest. Neither Gilmore's revolver nor his ammunition was at fault.

The sword had won the day this time, but such cases became fewer and fewer as the war continued. Revolvers emerged as the most efficient weapon for mounted combat, and breechloading, repeating carbines used after dismount often prevented an enemy from getting close enough for hand-to-hand combat. A number of famous Confederate cavalry units, including Mosby's Rangers, discarded sabers altogether, while Union horsemen fought increasingly on foot, using their mounts only as transportation from one battlefield to another.

The cavalry was probably most affected by the growing use of revolvers. Troopers usually carried one—sometimes two or more. All officers normally carried them, as did some enlisted men with the field artillery. Selected seamen also had them, and many infantry privates, especially during their first few months in the service, thrust personal handguns through their belts.

Yet, it is worth noting that the government did not manufacture revolvers in any of its armories. When civil war broke out in 1861, the official government-made handgun was the Springfield pistol-carbine adopted in 1855. A long weapon with a rifled barrel and detachable shoulder stock, it shot more accurately at longer ranges than the average pistol. And it used the patented Maynard

Rogers/Spencer .44-caliber revolver. Originally manufactured between 1863 and 1865 in Utica, New York. —Navy Arms

primer, invented by a Washington dentist and strongly recommended by Jefferson Davis, who had been secretary of war when the pistol was adopted. This ingenious primer, a tape encased with small dots of percussion compound, automatically fed over the nipple when the hammer was cocked, similar in fashion to toy cap pistols. In actual use, however, failure plagued it. Also, firing the weapon with the shoulder stock attached or detached affected its accuracy greatly. Troopers lost confidence in the pistol-carbine. After manufacturing slightly more than four thousand of these guns in 1856-57, the government ceased production.

In 1861 the Union army needed revolvers for its rapidly expanding cavalry—and it needed them fast. Almost anything that could shoot was welcome. Agents abroad purchased handguns in France and England while federal, state, and private buyers besieged American manufacturers. Designs for percussion revolvers, pin-fire revolvers and even a few rim-fire and center-fire cartridge revolvers abounded. Some were excellent arms; others were so impractical that only a wartime emergency allowed them to get into

production at all—and even that emergency could not make them a success.

Authorities differ about the number of pistol models carried by the Union troops either as official issue or as personal arms—a modest estimate is fifty different makes. The most conservative lists cite twenty as "primary martial," meaning those handguns purchased and issued by the federal government. Other pistols were classified as either "secondary martial"—those not made under specific government contracts—or "personal."

Ordnance officers charged with supplying ammunition for such a variety of weapons might well have given up in despair, but the reality was not so bad as it sounds since many of these models were bought in such small quantities that they were little more than curiosities. Colt and Remington revolvers made up almost 75 percent of all handguns purchased and issued by the government; adding the Starr models, in both single- and double-action, rises this figure to slightly more than 85 percent. All other pistol makes, therefore, comprised less than 15 percent of the total.

Most of the martial pistols were made in two calibers—the .44 (Army) and the .36 (Navy). These designations did not necessarily apply to the users, though—some soldiers preferred the .36 because they liked the feel of the grip and its lighter weight, while some sailors eagerly sought the .44 because of its greater power. Of the two calibers, the popular Army .44s outnumbered the Navy .36s by about ten to one. More Colt and Remington .44-caliber revolvers were purchased and issued by U.S. Ordnance than any other handgun. The Colt Army Model 1860 topped the list with a total of 128,697; the Remington counterpart followed with 115,563. In addition, huge quantities of both were bought by states and individuals.

An excellent handgun, the Colt Army appeared just in time to take advantage of the wartime demand. Prior to this, the pistols Colt first made for the Army were huge, heavy "dragoons," beginning with the famous Walker Colt in 1847. Through the years this monster came down in size, but it was not until the model 1860 appeared that a radically lighter and more streamlined version became available. It met with instantaneous success and, with the beginning of the war, began to set sales records.

The Remington, too, was a fine weapon. Many modern collectors consider it superior to the Colt, preferring its solid top strap over the frame to the "open top" of the Colt. Besides adding strength, the Remington's grooved top strap over

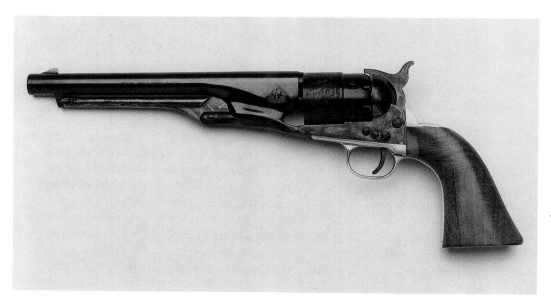

1860 Colt Army .44-caliber revolver. A very popular handgun with the Union forces. —EuroArms of America

1860 Colt Army .44-caliber revolver. —National Rifle Association

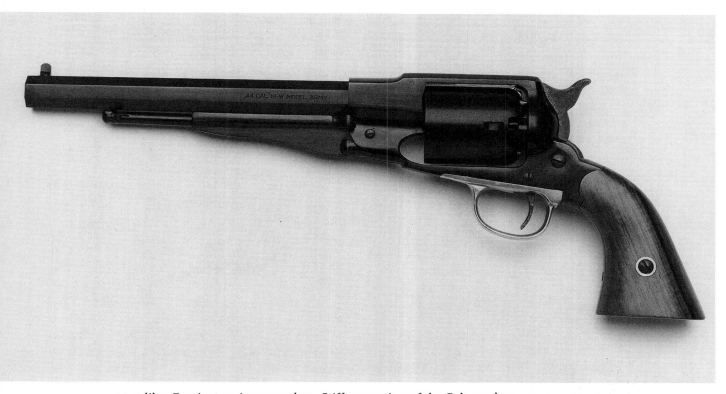

.44-caliber Remington Army revolver. Stiff competitor of the Colt revolver. —EuroArms of America

1851 Colt Navy .36-caliber revolver. A popular handgun during the Civil War. —Colt Firearms

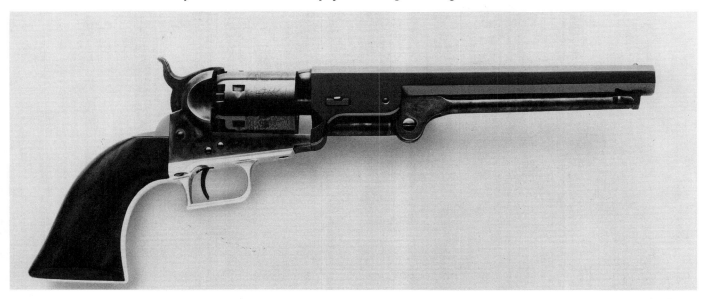

the cylinder served as a rear sight; the Colt's rear sight—a groove filed on the lip of the hammer—worked only when in the cocked position. Since a moving rear sight is not apt to be as accurate as a fixed one, the Remington, collectors say, has an advantage over the Colt in this respect.

But soldiers who used the two guns disagree. The ordnance chiefs' field reports generally favor the Colt and show mixed reactions to the Remington. Surprisingly, the soldiers considered the Colt stronger, despite its lack of a top strap, and criticized the Remington's tendency to get out of order. They called it dangerous to carry because it had no safety notch.

Most popular of the smaller caliber Colts was the Navy Model 1851. Despite this, the government bought only 11,696 of them—very few in contrast to the number of .44s purchased. Though lighter, the weapon's angular design made it seem bigger when compared with its streamlined Army counterpart. The 1861 model copied the smooth design of the .44. It is a fine and beauti-

fully balanced gun, but it failed to win favor from the government, which purchased only 2,363 of them. In design, the Remington Navy also ran well behind the Army version upon which it was modeled, but its total of 13,101 sales almost equaled the combined sales of the two Colt Navy revolvers.

Similar to the Remington Navy was the .36-caliber Whitney, manufactured by Eli Whitney Jr., son of the inventor of the cotton gin. Its solid frame did not prevent soldiers from damning it as a frail arm that got easily out of order. The government bought about 11,000, one of which almost killed Secretary of State William H. Seward on the night of Lincoln's assassination. Here its weak construction probably saved Seward's life: the frame bent when the attacker used the Whitney earlier as a club, and the gun failed to fire when he reached Seward's bedroom.

As percussion revolvers, these Colts, Remingtons, and Whitneys were loaded with prepared combustible cartridges inserted from

.44-caliber Remington Army "Stainless Steel" revolver. Union handgun. —Armsport

the front of the cylinders and pushed home with a loading lever pivoting from beneath the barrel. Each cartridge encased a bullet and a charge of powder wrapped in paper and collodion, which burns readily when primed by a spark. The spark, actually a jet of flame, came from a percussion cap placed on a nipple at the rear of each cylinder's chamber. All of these revolvers were single-action six-shooters with rifled barrels.

The Starr revolvers offered some variations not common on the most popular makes. Inventor E.T. Starr of New York City designed three models, two of which were double-action, eliminating the need to cock the hammer before shooting. But Starr's double-action Army and Navy models were soon abandoned in favor of his single-action Army model. Perhaps the trigger pull of the self-cocking type had been too long and heavy to suit the ordnance experts' tastes, or maybe they weren't yet ready for this technological advance.

Other designers also made double-action pistols. Government agents bought the Adams and Kerr five-shot, double-action percussion revolvers in England before and the Massachusetts Arms Company began manufacturing them in the United States. The Cooper, which copied the Colt in almost all other features, was also double action. C.S. Pettingill, of New Haven, invented a self-cocking "hammerless" revolver, later improved on by Edward Raymond and Charles Robitaille of Brooklyn. Its little L-shaped striker was completely enclosed. Each pull on the trigger revolved the cylinder, fired the gun, then cocked the striker for the next shot. Unfortunately it was too delicate a mechanism for field conditions, and the invisible hammer made it dangerous to carry. Another variant, the Savage, used two triggers—one for revolving the cylinder and cocking the hammer, the other for firing. Savage made three .36-caliber models that all worked on this principle.

The most advanced designs, however, came from France. Some French revolvers fired metallic cartridges, eliminating the need for a separate percussion cap. But ammunition for these was hard to come by, and European bore diameters varied from those commonly used in America. So few of these weapons made it to the Civil War arena that they had little effect. More common were the LeFauchoux pin-fire revolvers, about 12,000 of which the U.S. government bought. These .41-caliber double-action arms fired cartridges with short pins protruding just above their bases. When struck by the hammer, the pin drove into the internal primer and set it off. Unfortunately, the pin could be struck by accident with the same result when the cartridge was not in the gun, which made a soldier with a pouch full of these somewhat nervous. Nevertheless, the men who used these guns generally gave them good reports.

The next most common French cartridge revolvers were the Raphael and the Perrin. The Raphael was a .41-caliber double-action that used center-fire cartridges. Although almost a thousand Raphaels were purchased early during the war, any record of what happened to them after they reached this country is apparently lost, along with any reports on their performance. The Perrin, another double-action revolver, used a .45-caliber rim-fire cartridge; but only two hundred of these were purchased—too few for a field test.

Americans also made cartridge revolvers. By 1861 Smith & Wesson had begun production of its .22-caliber Model I and .32-caliber Model II. Both were small for military use, but many soldiers who preferred the easy-to-use rim-fire cartridges over the more cumbersome cap-and-ball weapons purchased them. Because Smith & Wesson controlled the American patent for a cylinder with the chambers bored all the way through—an essential feature in cartridge revolvers—no other U.S. firms could make them.

So, percussion-cap handguns reigned throughout the Civil War as the standard arm. Both Colt and Remington had fine, well-established revolvers that assured them dominance in the field. To catch the buyers' attention, new companies and inventors had to offer some feature they could claim as an improvement. Their efforts may have made life miserable for ordnance officers and armorers, but the abundance of trial models provides many delightful examples of mechanical ingenuity for modern collectors.

1858 Remington New Army .44-caliber. —Armsport

1851 Colt Navy .36-caliber. One of the best known cap-and-ball revolvers. —Connecticut Valley Arms

Handguns of the Confederacy

Confederate soldiers sometimes went into battle unarmed. Officers cursed as they struggled with revolvers that wouldn't fire. But the South fought on stubbornly. In the aftermath cavalrymen searched the battlefields for dead men's guns, arming themselves with whatever came to hand.

They prized their guns as they prized their lives, and every man tried desperately to acquire extra arms. One pistol might malfunction, a second might be lost in battle, but if a man had three or four, he could face the enemy without stopping even to reload. Some of these men, such as those who rode with Lt. David Smith Terry as Terry's Texas Rangers, became self-contained arsenals, carrying two guns in holsters on their belts and two more in saddle holsters.

The Confederacy ingeniously solved the problem of providing enough pistols to meet the demand, even with limited facilities. They used captured parts to make new pistol-carbines. Copying the designs of Colts, Remingtons, and Whitneys—with brass parts because of the iron shortage—men became gun manufactures overnight. Two men even invented new pistols: Thomas Coffer built a gun with a two-piece cylinder that was more or less a cross between the percussion and cartridge system; and Jean LeMat made one of the deadliest weapons of the war—the famous "grapeshot" revolver—with one barrel in .36- or .42-caliber and a second one that spewed a .60-caliber charge of shot.

At the outbreak of the war the North became flooded with different kinds of guns. Union ordnance officers were plagued by the diversity as government revolver purchases soared to the hundreds of thousands. Confederate ordnance officers had problems too, but of an exactly opposite nature. Material shortages and scarce machinery limited the South's revolver production to only tens of thousands.

A few handguns were made in the South before the outbreak of the war, but these were mostly single-shot percussion pistols. It remained easy to obtain revolvers directly from northern makers right up to the start of hostilities; by then, a number of southern states and many individuals had acquired their basic supplies. When war broke out, the first troops in the field carried these northern guns, along with older models and some imported English models. The Yankees also obliged by leaving many weapons on the fields of battle during the early years of successful Confederate campaigns.

The South's capture of the federal arsenal at Harpers Ferry in April 1861 provided a wealth of parts that the Rebels joyously took to Fayetteville, North Carolina, where they assembled a Confederate version of the clumsy 1855 pistol-carbine. It differed from its Union counterpart most noticeably in that it omitted the Maynard-tape primer. Although Jefferson Davis, president of the Confederacy, had been impressed with this primer, his ordnance officers were not, and their decision carried. The Fayetteville pistol-carbines were no more popular than the original 1855 model; but guns were scarce, and there was no point in letting them go to waste. After the parts were used up, production stopped. The military realized it needed regular revolvers.

The Confederacy offered amazing inducements to get new arms into production. It offered arms-factory workers deferment from active service and financed factory set-up costs. If federal troops captured the plant, the debt would be cancelled. Self-proclaimed manufacturers, willing in spirit, were not in short supply. Unfortunately, few had the necessary experience and ability.

Of the many contractors who signed agreements to produce as many as 15,000 revolvers each within three years, only five succeeded in making any substantive contribution. These were Griswold & Gunnison, Leech & Rigdon, Rigdon & Ansley, Spiller & Burr, and the Columbus Firearms Company. Harassed by manufacturing problems, material shortages, a lack of skilled labor, and frequent moves to avoid Union troops, their combined production totaled less than 15,000 revolvers.

Interestingly, while Union soldiers preferred Colt's .44-caliber Army Model 1860, Southerners

1851 Colt Navy .36-caliber revolver. Southern copy of a Union handgun, using brass because of the South's iron shortage. —Armsport

Griswold & Gunnison .36-caliber Confederate handgun. —National Rifle Association

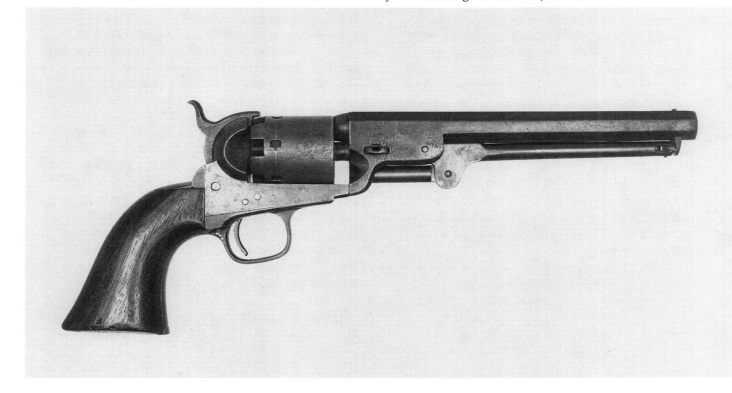

favored that maker's .36-caliber Navy Model 1851. Most of the Confederate-made handguns imitated it, though variations were made to simplify manufacture and to substitute available materials for those in short supply. Barrels, for instance, were almost always round instead of octagonal, as in the original Colt; recoil shields were sometimes omitted; and, in the case of the Griswold & Gunnison, the frame was made of brass instead of iron. These "Confederate Colts" can readily be recognized by such differences, as well as by a finish rougher than that on those made at the Colt factory.

One of the top five Confederate gun makers—Spiller & Burr of Richmond—chose the Whitney Navy revolver rather than the Colt as its model. The company encountered such production difficulties, however, that the Confederate States government finally bought it out and moved the machinery. Some of the Whitneys are marked "C.S." or "Spiller & Burr" or both; others bear no markings whatsoever. In any case, brass frames indicate manufacture in the South.

In addition to these "primary" revolvers made directly under contract to the Confederacy, there was a "secondary" group made for sale to private citizens. Most of these were made in Texas by such firms as Dance Brothers or Tucker, Sherrod & Company. Dance Brothers copied the Colt, but omitted its recoil shield and produced a distinctive flat frame. Tucker, Sherrod & Company usually copied the big Colt .44 dragoon of the prewar era.

Had these been the only Confederate guns made, this would be a story of woefully inefficient copies of Yankee revolvers. But there were two innovators who set out to make an improved product. Thomas W. Coffer of Portsmouth, Virginia, and Dr. Jean Alexander Francois LeMat of New Orleans added new dimensions to Southern gun design. Coffer attempted to build a cartridge revolver that would circumvent Smith & Wesson's patent, and LeMat devised the 10-shot percussion "grapeshot" revolver.

It seems odd that a gunsmith in a country at war should worry about a patent held by the enemy, but Coffer went to great lengths to avoid using the bored-through cylinder under patent to Smith & Wesson. He invented a two-piece cylinder: the forward section contained the chambers for the charges while the rear piece had smaller holes that could be lined up with the chambers. The forward chambers held special cartridges that had slender rearward projections, which the aft part of the cylinder slipped over so that the cartridge projections stuck through its smaller holes, much in the manner of the percussion caps on other revolvers. Loading the gun required removing the cylinder, an obvious inconvenience. More important, the metal shortage in the South made a cartridge arm impractical.

Few models of Coffer's ingenious arm were made before he gave up and began producing percussion revolvers with a standard cylinder. Those that were made had solid frames, like Whitneys and Remingtons but made of brass, and spur triggers without a guard. Specimens are extremely rare. Union forces captured Portsmouth in May 1862 and ended production of the Coffer revolver after an estimated total output of only fifty guns.

Dr. LeMat was more successful. Actually, he had received a patent for his revolver from the United States back in 1856, almost five years before the war broke out, and had tried without success to interest the federal government in it. Once the war began, however, he had no difficulty in obtaining a contract from the Confederacy and promptly set out for France, where he could manufactured his arms more easily and safely than in the South.

From all accounts, the LeMat was a very deadly weapon. Made in .44 caliber, its cylinder was bored for nine loads fired in the normal fashion through a rifled barrel. Immediately beneath this conventional barrel was a second, smoothbore, barrel of .65 caliber that could be loaded with buckshot and fired after turning down the nose of the hammer. This feature gave the pistol its nickname "grapeshot." At close range it proved deadly.

The LeMat was not only formidable, but reliable as well. The officers who tested it for the U.S. Army before the war had recommended it highly, even though no acquisition followed. Three Confederate generals—Pierre Gustave Toutant Beauregard, the colorful Confederate officer who directed the firing on Fort Sumter and who at one time had been LeMat's partner, Patton Anderson, and the dashing cavalry leader "Jeb" Stuart— carried LeMats. At the end of the war, when Jefferson Davis was captured by Union troops in his final dash for freedom and perhaps another try, he was reported to have been carrying a "ten-shot revolver"—undoubtedly one of LeMat's.

LeMat revolvers held nine rounds in .44-caliber with a .65-caliber center barrel, a total of ten shots. Top to bottom: Army, Navy, Cavalry. —Navy Arms

Rifled Muskets

Many historians often refer to the American Civil War as the first truly modern war. Not only did the conflict become the proving ground for military tactics never before tried on the battlefield, it also put to the test a great deal of modernized equipment, including the breechloading firearm. For the muzzleloading romanticist, however, the era could also be known as the last of the old wars, marking for this country, anyway, the end of the military's use for muzzleloading guns.

The big .58-caliber percussion muskets that saw their last large-scale use on the battlefield at Gettysburg, represent the final evolution of the front-loading military musket. None could not match the fire power of the Spencer and Henry repeaters, or even the single-shot Sharps for that matter. By the war's end, the breechloader had clearly established its superiority and potential to become the military arm of the future, but not before several million of the percussion rifled muskets had been used on the battlefield.

The Springfield Armory, in Springfield, Massachusetts, together with a number of private contractors, produced around 1.5 million .58-caliber percussion rifled muskets between 1861 and 1865. The ability to produce large numbers of military arms gave the Union forces a distinct advantage over the Confederacy. Even so, Union troops carried more than 400,000 of the British .575-caliber Enfield rifled muskets into battle. Additionally, the U.S. Ordnance Board approved the purchase of more than 700,000 various makes and models of rifled muskets and smoothbore muskets from makers in Austria, France, Belgium, and Germany. Ordnance was no problem.

The South was somewhat harder pressed to produce or procure enough arms for its troops. At the outbreak of the war most Confederate soldiers carried guns that had been captured from federal armories in the South, many of which were flintlock smoothbores converted to percussion arms. The first few years of the war even saw many true flintlock guns carried by Confederate troops. The capture of Harpers Ferry Arsenal on April 18, 1861, netted arms-making parts much needed by the South. Equipment captured during the raid was shipped to armories in Richmond, Fayetteville, and Ashville, where the South's major arms production took place.

Dozens of small armories across the South made valiant efforts to arm the troops, but they could not produce enough to outfit the more than 750,000 men that eventually served the southern cause. Most Confederate arms came either from

Two-Band Enfield .58-caliber rifle manufactured in Great Britain and purchased by the Confederacy during the Civil War in great quantities. —Dixie Gun Works

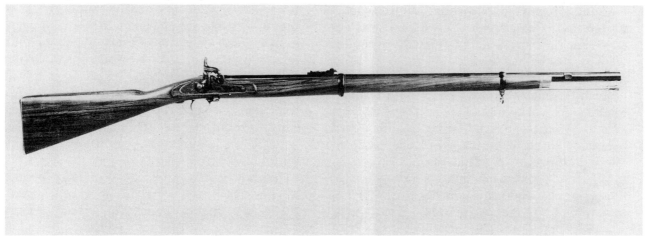

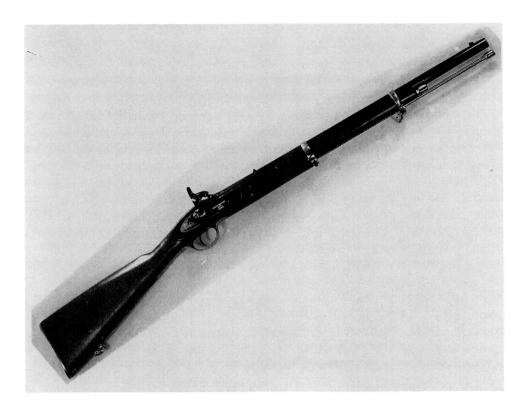

Cook & Brother .58-caliber Confederate carbine.
—*EuroArms of America*

battlefield recoveries or from the 300,000 long guns purchased in England, Austria, and Belgium, most of which were of the British Enfield design.

During the first years of the war, northern troops carried either the older Model 1855 or the newly adopted Model 1861 Springfield rifled muskets. The Model 1855 featured the Maynard-tape priming system that mechanically fed a metallic disk over the cone of the nipple as the hammer was drawn to full cock. This disk, attached to a rolled piece of paper much like caps for a toy cap gun, contained the priming charge for ignition. Though a clever system, it was not error-free and newer-model percussion nipples were capped by hand.

The Model 1861 Springfield rifled musket was basically a redesigned version of the .58-caliber Model 1855, without the Maynard-tape priming system. The new model still used the odd-shaped hammer, flat barrel bands, and barrel-band retaining springs of its predecessor. The Springfield Armory produced more than 265,000 of these, and about 500,000 more came from twenty or so private contractors, including Savage Arms

Company, Eli Whitney, and Providence Tool Company.

In 1863, the government-patterned Springfield musket received a facial uplift. The odd-shaped hammer that had been carried over from the Model 1855 was replaced with a more stylish, yet heftier S-shaped hammer. The solid, flat barrel bands were replaced with rounded bands that fastened in place with a screw across the bottom, eliminating the need for the band springs—or so it was thought. A modified version of the Model 1863, built in 1864, featured a solid upper and lower barrel band rounded in contour because the bands on the original version had a tendency to work loose after considerable use or when the musket was being fired at a sustained rate. On the revised model the middle barrel band was split at the bottom to attach the upper sling swivel. All three bands were held in place with retaining springs, reintroduced after their brief absence. All Model 1863 muskets were produced at the Springfield Armory.

Another very popular rifled musket was the Model 1861 Special. The design of this musket has been attributed to Colt, which produced just

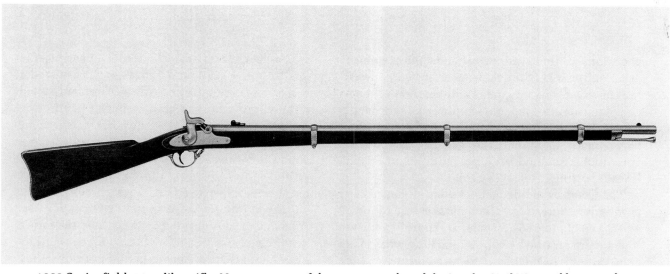

1863 Springfield .58-caliber rifle. Neary 274,000 of these were produced during the Civil War and became the stabilizers of the dreaded minié ball. —Navy Arms

over 100,000 of the percussion .58-caliber long arms during the war years. Two other firms also produced a large number of the Model 1861 Specials: Amoskeag Manufacturing Company turned out 27,000 Model 1861 Specials; and Lamson, Goodnow & Yale accounted for another 50,000. Although the 1861 Special looks a great deal like the 1863 Springfield, the two guns share few, if any, interchangeable parts. All the 1861 models, regardless of the maker, show extremely close tolerances and many parts interchange readily.

Many muzzleloading experts consider the Colt Model 1861 Special (and the 1861 Specials made by Amoskeag and Lamson, Goodnow & Yale) the finest muzzleloading military arm ever produced. The gun combines the streamlined look of the Springfield models and the tapered rifling of the highly accurate British Enfield muskets.

Had the war lasted much longer, the .575-caliber British-made Enfields might have become the most widely used arm during the conflict. Altogether, between 600,000 and 700,000 of the various Enfield patterns saw use by both North and South. The most popular style was the 1863 rifled musket. Compared to the American-made Civil War muskets, the Enfields were highly finished arms. Though U.S. manufacturers

Top to bottom: three-band Enfield, two-band Enfield, and Enfield musketoon. These were favorites of the Confederate calvalry. —EuroArms of America

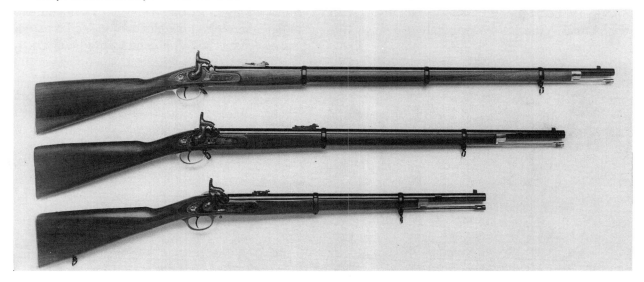

occasionally blued the barrel bands, the barrels of practically all U.S. muskets were buffed and left in the white; the lock plates and hammers generally, but not always, came color-case hardened. But the Enfields sported deeply blued barrels and barrel bands, brilliant color-case hardened locks, and stocks finished on a par with some of the finest sporting arms of the time.

The firearms reviewed here were all definitely long guns. American rifled muskets in Models 1861, 1863, and 1861 Special all sported a forty-inch tapered round barrel, an inch longer than the 1863 Enfield. All of these American front-loading military muskets featured three-grooved rifling designed to shoot the big, hollow-based conical slugs designed by French Capt. Claude Étienne Minié. The Enfield and the Model 1861 Special featured rifling grooves cut about .015 inch at the breech and tapering to .005 inch at the muzzle. The two models were extremely accurate for having such large bores. And, their payloads hit like a ton of bricks.

The standard service load carried by troops north and south in the Civil War consisted of 60 grains of FFg black powder behind a minié ball weighing approximately 500 grains. The cartridges generally were prepackaged in nitrated paper. To load, the shooter either ripped or bit off the end of the paper cartridge, poured the powder into the barrel, then rammed the remaining paper and bullet down the bore. Upon firing, the hot flash of the burning powder totally consumed the nitrated paper. A soldier could carry about forty rounds in a leather cartridge box with a shoulder strap. The cartridges saved him from fumbling for separate powder charges and bullets. The guns still had to be capped by hand or by means of a mechanical, hand-held capping device.

The American minié ball designed for the Models 1861, 1863, and 1861 Special featured a long ogive—a slender nose projecting from the tip of the larger-diameter conical bullet. Encircling the basal portion of the bullet were three grooves that helped hold the paper cartridge to the slug; when fired, they engaged the rifling and scraped fouling from the bore. Lubrication of some sort might have been used in these grooves. When loading bullets without the aid of a paper cartridge, most soldiers simply lubricated the minié by spitting into its hollow base. Of course, they did this only in the heat of battle; normally they used a wax-tallow mixture to lubricate bullets.

The .575 Enfields were designed to shoot hollow-based Pritchett bullets, slightly smaller in diameter than the miniés. When Pritchetts weren't available, the tighter-fitting .577-inch-diameter U.S. minié bullets were commonly fired in the Enfields, often requiring considerable sizing before they could be loaded. The Enfields' great accuracy is often attributed using the tight-fitting miniés in place of the Pritchetts.

Introduction of the hollow-based minié ball accounts largely for the switch to rifled arms by all the world's military powers. Patch-clad round balls took too much time to load in a rifled arm during battle, and they fouled the bore quickly. But the big, hollow-based, cylindrical miniés—slightly smaller than the bore size for quicker loading—did not require patching. Instead, the shooter dropped a bullet down the muzzle and seated it directly over the powder charge. Upon ignition, expanding gases from the powder charge flared the thin walls of the bullet's hollow base into the bore's wide rifling grooves. Accuracy of the big slugs in a quality musket achieved new heights, and big muzzleloaders could be loaded twice as fast as with patched round balls.

CHAPTER 3

NON-MILITARY ARMS

The Imitated Pistol

Imitation, it has been said, is the sincerest form of flattery. If this is so, Henry Deringer Jr. must have been one of the most sincerely flattered gun makers in history. Other gunsmiths throughout America copied his designs, imitated his workmanship, and even pirated his name and trademark. Within his lifetime Deringer's name became a common noun that applied to a whole class of firearms. No other U.S. gun maker ever achieved such distinction.

Deringer's famous product was a pistol, more specifically, a short-barreled pocket pistol in a large and powerful caliber. The concept did not strike him suddenly, as in a flash of insight, but it developed over a number of years as part of his regular line of gun making.

Born the son of a gunsmith in 1786 in Easton, Pennsylvania, young Henry Deringer Jr. was apprenticed to his father's trade in Richmond, Virginia. In 1806 he moved to Philadelphia and set up his own business. Mostly, he made muskets and rifles for individuals on special order and for the U.S. government on contract. He also made a few handguns—flintlocks at first, then percussion models. Deringer's dueling pistols (and other guns, too) achieved renown for their high quality; but he was known in his early years primarily as a maker of shoulder arms.

In 1825 Deringer began concentrating his skill on handguns, though not yet on very small models. In that year, he made a pair of percussion pistols for Maj. Francis W. Armstrong, who worked closely with soon-to-be-president Andrew Jackson on a policy to remove eastern Indians to reservations west of the Mississippi River and, in 1831, was appointed by Jackson as the Choctaw agent. The pistols Deringer made for Armstrong were probably the type collectors now call "greatcoat" or "coaching" pistols. They quickly attracted attention and Deringer's name became recognized as a symbol of pistol quality. In succeeding years he turned his attention increasingly to such arms.

The pocket pistol that brought Deringer his greatest fame probably did not debut until 1848 or 1849, when the veteran gun maker was in his sixties. He had developed the distinctive style gradually: the back-action lock, with the firing mechanism set into the wood behind the hammer rather than in front of it, first appeared perhaps in the mid-1830s; the foliate engraving and trademark "DERINGER/PHILADELPHIA" appeared by the early 1840s; meanwhile, the checkered grips and large hammer spur had also become characteristic of his work. Other traits that made his pistols distinct evolved perhaps as gradually; among them are the small size, the "bird's-head"

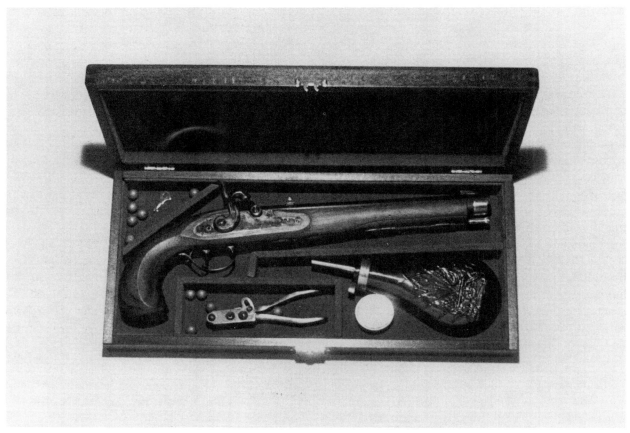

.44-caliber Kentucky percussion pistol. Except for ignition, this design remained unchanged from pre-1830 models. —Navy Arms

contour of the butt, and the unique barrel—flat-topped for its entire length and octagonal at the rear with the sides and bottom rounded near the muzzle.

When the classic Deringer finally appeared, it was a deadly little weapon. The barrel length varied from 27/32 to 4 inches, with overall pistol lengths of 3 3/4 inches for vest-pocket models to the greatcoat, measuring 9 inches. Calibers ranged from .33 to .51. The barrels were always rifled with seven grooves twisting in a clockwise direction. Black walnut stocks and German silver mountings, except for a few extra-fancy guns with gold and gold-plated mountings, completed the Deringer's styling. Henry Deringer regarded barrel construction and decoration significant characteristics that separated genuine specimens, made

in his own shop, from imitations. The wrought iron barrels were etched and browned in swirls to simulate a Damascus twist. The muzzles sported very low blade sights, and sometimes he added a raised notch sight at the rear.

The little pistol packed a man-sized punch. Accuracy for the shortest specimens might be limited to six or seven feet, but deadly all the same. Their size was such that they could be easily concealed, usually fitting into a pocket with scarcely a wrinkle showing. Some men fastened them inside their waistcoats, tied them in their coat sleeves, stuck them in their boots, or even hid them down the backs of their collars. Women also had a variety of hiding places for them. Deringer's pistols would fit almost anywhere, ready for any short-ranged emergency. Here was a wonderful weapon for the person who wished to appear unarmed, but knew better than to go without a gun. They served well as hideout weapons in case one had to surrender an unconcealed arm to an adversary.

Despite its many advantages, it took a number of years for the Deringer to achieve wide acceptance. Sales grew through the early 1850s, reaching a peak in the six years prior to the Civil War, with a total of about 8,000 pistols sold. By then, imitators brazenly copied Henry Deringer's style and even his name. To avoid lawsuits, some of his competitors called their guns "derringers," spelling the name differently to sidestep trademark infringement.

The Civil War and the advent of breechloaders brought a decline to the derringer, but in its brief heyday, the little pistol gained much attention. Its greatest markets were in the South and West, especially in California Territory, where the Army and Navy Journal reported: "The sharp crack of the Deringer . . . was heard in the land much more frequently than the voice of the turtle." Almost

everyone in the territory—gamblers, lawmen, newspaper editors, politicians, and just plain citizens—seemed to carry one, sometimes two. Derringers played a role in one homicide after another ranging from murders of anonymous miners in gold fields to the murder on Feb. 27, 1859, of Phillip Barton Key, the son of Francis Scott Key, by Congressman Daniel Sickles within a stone's throw of the White House. Six years later came the most notorious of these murders—the assassination of Abraham Lincoln by John Wilkes Booth. Everyone in the country came to know Deringer's name from reading about these crimes in the newspapers.

When Henry Deringer died in 1868 at the age of eighty-one, he was a wealthy man, highly respected in his community. By then, cartridge guns had nearly driven his percussion pistol off the market, but his idea of a small pocket gun with a large bore had been accepted all over the country. And these arms were—and still are—called derringers, even though the later ones utilize self-contained ammunition.

Arms for Assassination

On April 9, 1865, Gen. Robert E. Lee surrendered on behalf of the Confederate States of America at Appomattox Courthouse. Five days later the jubilation in Washington was still at its height as crowds thronged the city celebrating the return of peace. It was Good Friday, April 14; the air was filled with thanksgiving. That night, a single pistol shot brought down the North from unbounded joy to bottomless grief. With the aid of a small band of conspirators, a deluded actor named John Wilkes Booth shot and fatally wounded the president of the United States.

For weeks previously, Booth and his accomplices had been developing their plans and collecting arms. The original idea was not to kill Lincoln, but to take him captive and perhaps

exchange him for a whole army of Confederate prisoners of war. After Appomattox negated that possibility, Booth set his sights on assassination. At the same time, he expanded the target list to include Vice President Andrew Johnson, Secretary of State William H. Seward, and possibly General Ulysses S. Grant.

The conspirators acquired a miscellany of arms, good weapons all. The lot included a .45-caliber Deringer percussion pistol mounted in German silver and containing a cap box in its butt—a small but deadly gun of excellent quality made by Deringer himself in his Philadelphia factory; two Colts—a .36-caliber Navy Model 1851 and a .44-caliber Army model 1860—both six-shot percussion revolvers; and a Whitney .36-caliber Navy percussion revolver. Two cartridge arms rounded out the lot, both were seven-shot .52-caliber Spencer repeating carbines that loaded through a magazine in the butt. Deringer pistols had long been prized for their fine workmanship and their deadliness at close range; Colt revolvers were the most popular handguns of the war; and the Spencer carbines had won universal praise from soldiers as the best repeating arms in the service. This arsenal was impressive.

In addition to the guns, the conspirators had gathered a number of knives, three of which were of the "bowie" type suited to heavy fighting or general utility. The bowie knives were English-made with antler grips and spear-pointed blades. The one that figured most prominently in the conspiracy was manufactured by W.F. Jackson of Sheffield, and bore the stamped inscription: RIO GRANDE CAMP KNIFE. Also in the deadly collection was an English folding pocket dagger.

On the night of the assassination President and Mrs. Lincoln had gone to Ford's Theater to see "Our American Cousin," starring Laura Keene. General and Mrs. Grant were to have accompanied them, but at the last minute they decided to go to New Jersey instead to visit their children. Their places were taken by Clara Harris, daughter of U.S. Senator Ira Harris of New York, and her fiance, Maj. Henry R. Rathbone.

The party sat in the state box, with President Lincoln occupying a rocking chair at the left, Mrs. Lincoln to his right, then Major Rathbone and Miss Harris. Flags and an engraving of George Washington decorated the box. A small access door from the corridor was directly behind the president; no one noticed the small peep hole bored through it, which permitted a view of the occupants of the box and the action on stage. Another door allowed main access to the box, and through it the Lincoln party had entered.

At about 10:15 p.m. Booth struck. Entering the box silently, he fired the Deringer pointblank at the president's head. The bullet entered the skull midway between the left ear and the mid-line of the back of the head, and lodged directly behind the right eye. Lincoln, who was leaning toward the stage with his hand on the rail, slumped forward, then fell back unconscious. Major Rathbone sprang at the assassin; Booth dropped this pistol, drew the camp knife, and wounded the major in the left arm. Eluding the officer's grasp, Booth clung to the railing and slashed toward the major as Rathbone tried again to seize him, then he vaulted over the railing to the stage below. Rathbone's effort prevented Booth from clearing the railing cleanly, causing his right boot to strike the engraving of Washington and catching his spur in one of the flags. He lost his balance and fell heavily to the stage, breaking his left leg. Despite the injury, he managed to struggle to his feet. He brandished the knife and shouted, *Sic semper tyrannis*," before escaping. On his way out he slashed at the orchestra leader, cutting his clothes, then, using the butt of the knife, felled a boy holding the horse on which he escaped.

Booth managed to evade capture, even though he stopped to pick up one of the Spencer carbines he had hidden at Lloyd's Tavern in Surrattsville, Maryland. He also had with him both Colt revolvers and the folding dagger. These weapons were found in his possession when he was cornered and shot in Garrets barn, near Bowling Green, Virginia, on the morning of April 26, nearly two weeks later.

Of the other assassinations scheduled to occur that night, only one was attempted. The man assigned to attack the vice president lost his nerve, but Lewis Powell almost succeeded in murdering the secretary of state, who was confined to bed recovering from a carriage accident that left him with a broken jaw and fractured vertebrae. Powell—or Payne, as he called himself at the time—came to Seward's door as a messenger bringing medicine from the secretary's doctor. He carried a knife and the Whitney revolver. The ruse worked on the servant, but then things went awry. Near the top of the stairs, Frederick Seward, the secretary's oldest son, met the would-be assassin and refused to let him enter his father's bedroom. After a brief argument, Powell struck young Seward with the butt of his revolver, fracturing his skull and knocking him senseless. Fortunately for Frederick, the gun's loading lever broke and the cylinder pin bent so that it could not be fired.

Powell felled a soldier-nurse who stepped out of the sick room, then knocked down a second attendant and leaped on the secretary.

The steel framework Seward's doctor had placed his patient's neck to hold the broken bones in place saved his life. In the dark room and amidst all the excitement, Powell succeeded only in gashing Seward's face and shoulders. Then help arrived and the assassin's opportunity was gone.

Powell fought his way out of the house with his knife, leaving the useless revolver on the floor. Captured later in the evening, he was hanged with the other conspirators.

All the plotters' weapons were put in evidence at the trial that promptly followed. Most have been in government ownership ever since. The National Park Service keeps them on permanent display in Washington, D.C., at Ford's Theater.

Guns of the War Chiefs

Geronimo. Sitting Bull. These and other Indian warriors achieved reputations that sent chills down the spines of even the bravest frontiersmen. They became symbols of bloodthirsty battle, death, and destruction to all who opposed them. They led some of the fiercest fighters the world has ever known. Few warring groups have ever aroused so much interest and curiosity as the fighting Indians of the American West.

From dime novels to Wild West shows to motion pictures, legend (and Hollywood) has lumped all native Americans—Apache, Sioux, Pawnee, Ute, and dozens more—together into one anonymous mounted warrior in a feathered war bonnet, invariably sporting a gun (supplied by some whiskey-peddling white trader) better than the arms of the soldiers and settlers he fought. The facts have been slow in debunking this myth and presenting Indians as they really were, with their rich variety of customs, dress, and attitudes. A truer picture is gradually emerging of their weapons as well.

Guns were scarce and highly prized by Indians in the Old West. Muzzleloading flintlocks remained most popular until the latter decades of the nineteenth century, when more modern arms and metallic cartridges began showing up on the frontier. The repeating carbines so commonly seen in the hands of movie Indians were in reality treasures worthy of fighting chiefs. Short-barreled lever-action rifles were valued for their light

weight, easy handling, and capacity to shoot repeatedly without delay.

A few of the weapons seized during the final major uprisings belonged to the greatest Indian leaders in American history. Some, such as the Winchester .44 carbine that belonged to Sitting Bull, are on display in the Smithsonian Institution, in Washington, D.C.; others are in collections such as that in the Heye Foundation's Museum of the American Indian in New York City.

Sitting Bull

Probably the most powerful chief of all the Plains Indians was Sitting Bull of the Hunkpapa Sioux. A warrior who counted his first coup at the age of fourteen, he later became a highly respected medicine man and tribal councilor. Sitting Bull, along with Crazy Horse of the Oglala Sioux, organized several thousand Sioux, Cheyennes, and Arapahoes who went on the warpath in 1876 to protest white invasion of the Black Hills. In June Crazy Horse defeated Gen. George Crook at the Rosebud River. A week later the combined force wiped out Custer's command at the Little Big Horn. Although often pictured as a fighter, Sitting Bull rarely appeared on the battlefield and seldom fired a gun; instead, he acted from behind the lines as councilor and strategist.

Faced with increasing pressure from the army, Sitting Bull and his followers retreated to Canada after their bout with the Seventh Cavalry. Gradually, hunger and despair forced them back to reservations in the United States. Sitting Bull surrendered to Maj. David Brotherton at Fort Buford, Dakota Territory, on July 21, 1881. He remained at peace, and even worked with Buffalo Bill Cody's Wild West Show for a while, but was suspected in the late 1880s of stirring up trouble among some tribal factions. In 1890, he was shot and killed by Indian police who claimed he resisted arrest. The gun that Brotherton took from Sitting Bull was a .44 Winchester repeating carbine, Model 1866, bearing the traditional Indian decoration of brass-headed tacks.

Chief Joseph

One of the greatest Indian military leaders of all time, Chief Joseph led his band of Nez Perce on a thousand-mile flight through mountainous terrain from Idaho to Yellowstone Park, then across Montana toward Canada after the army decided to restrict them to their reservation in 1877. Along the way, Joseph and his forces defeated or outwitted four army columns, some commanded by famous Civil War officers. His warriors, estimated at no more than one or two hundred, repelled superior troops in at least a dozen engagements. Gen. Oliver Otis Howard followed close behind the refugees every step of their way. Joseph's feat has been compared with some of the greatest organized retreats in history.

After four long months, Gen. Nelson A. Miles finally besieged Joseph's weary band in the Bear Paw Mountains of Montana, only thirty miles from the safety of the Canadian border. Indian messengers managed to get past the army lines and reach Sitting Bull, who was already in Canada. They asked for his help, but it was no use. On October 5, 1877, the Nez Perce surrendered and Joesph made his famous speech, telling General Howard ". . . from where the sun now stands, I will fight no more forever."

Miles called Chief Joseph "the highest type of Indian I have ever known, very handsome, kind and brave." Though the Nez Perce were widely praised for sparing lives and causing minimal damage, Joseph was exiled to Indian Territory (Oklahoma) for many years before returning to his people on the Colville Reservation in Washington. He died there in 1904. The rifle Chief Joseph surrendered to Generals Miles and Howard was a .45/60 Kennedy repeater, an octogonal-barreled lever-action gun manufactured by the Whitney Arms Company.

Nahce

Son of the famed Cochise, who died in 1874, Nahce (sometimes spelled Naiche or Nai-chi-ti) was hereditary chief of the Chiricahua Apaches for whom Geronimo was medicine man. The name Nahce, appropriately enough, means "mischief." To the white settlers of Arizona and New Mexico, he was that and more.

Nahce was one of the most resourceful Indians, leading the Chiricahuas on depredations in the southwestern United States and northern Mexico until they were finally subdued by General Miles in 1886. The war chief was imprisoned and, even after his release, kept under constant, close surveillance. He became a peaceful leader of his people until he died on the Mescalero Reservation in New Mexico in 1921. The gun Nahce surrendered at Fort Bowie, Arizona Territory, in 1886 was a lever-action carbine, a .45/60 Winchester repeater, Model 1876.

Geronimo

Geronimo was a medicine man and prophet of the Chiricahuas. His name became so famous as a symbol of warlike ferocity that United States paratroopers adopted it as their battle cry. Contrary to popular belief, however, Geronimo was not a chief; he was a leader and councilor of the Chiricahuas, while Cochise, then Nahce, actually served as their chiefs. Throughout the 1870s and 1880s, the army made strenuous attempts to subdue and pacify the Apaches of Arizona. Intermittently, the soldiers succeeded; but then the Indians would suddenly leave their reservations to terrorize whites in the Southwest, often crossing the border to take refuge in Mexico. A warrior as well as a medicine man, Geronimo often led the raiding parties.

In 1882, he surrendered to Gen. George Crook, and for a while became a peaceful (and successful) farmer. But in 1885 he returned to the warpath for his last campaign. For eighteen months he consistently eluded more than 5,500 troops until, on September 5, 1886, he surrendered to General Miles. He was shipped forthwith from prison to prison on various army posts. Although he was eventually freed, he spent the rest of his life under close watch. He died at Fort Sill, Oklahoma, in 1909.

Geronimo had many guns. The one he presented to Crook during the aborted 1886 peace conferences in northern Mexico, was a .45/60 Winchester repeating carbine, Model 1876.

Rain-in-the-Face

The West still vividly remembers the blood bath that took place when the Sioux war parties gathered under Rain-in-the-Face, a chief of the Hunkpapa Sioux. An almost implacable enemy of the white man, he participated in two of the most devastating battles ever fought against troops sent to guard the frontier: the 1866 Fetterman Massacre in Wyoming and the infamous defeat of Custer's Seventh Cavalry in Montana a decade later—both unequivocal victories for the Indians. Many have claimed that Rain-in-the-Face personally killed Custer; no evidence supports this assertion, and the warrior himself always denied it.

Like many of the other Indian leaders, Rain-in-the-Face eventually realized he was fighting a hopeless war. He had never been one to give up, but he saw that ultimate victory for his people was impossible. After surrendering in 1880, he remained at peace until he died in 1905. The gun he surrendered to General Miles at Fort Keogh, Montana Territory, in 1880 was a single-shot .52-caliber Sharps breechloading carbine. Its hammer was missing. There is no record of whether the rifle was in this condition when Rain-in-the-Face surrendered, but if so, he might have deliberately chosen a worthless weapon as his surrender gun.

Indian Trade Guns

An enduring tale that every gun enthusiast hears sooner or later concerns the arms traded to Indians by early fur buyers. According to this fable, an Indian could obtain a gun by trading a stack of beaver pelts equal in height to the length of the gun. This story has been spread for years and is sheer nonsense.

Though Indians valued any firearm, they did not prefer the long, heavy rifles often used by fur traders. Instead, they wanted light guns they could handle easily and carry all day without tiring. They preferred smoothbores over rifles because they were easier to use and could be adapted to a variety of purposes. Rifles had to be loaded carefully with patched ball, and their bores fouled quickly with powder residue. Indians were not noted for the care they gave their guns and seldom cleaned the barrels. Also, rifles had comparatively small bores and could not hold enough shot for hunting small game. Smoothbores, on the other hand, could shoot single balls or buckshot.

To meet the requirements fur men submitted to trading companies for guns they could easily trade to the Indians for pelts, gun makers developed a special type of gun. Collectors have given it many names—Northwest gun, Hudson's Bay Fuke, Mackinaw gun, Indian musket, or simply trade gun. All models used flintlock mechanisms and barrels of about .58 caliber that ranged from thirty to forty-two inches in length. They first appeared early in the 1700s and continued almost without change until 1850.

These were the Indians' favorite guns for more than a hundred years. They preferred them over the newer percussion-cap and cartridge arms because the caps and cartridges were available only through traders and at great cost; however, Indians could easily obtaining flints for their trade guns. And flintlocks were easier to load—even on horseback—than percussion arms. Placing the tiny percussion cap on a nipple was a delicate operation; but with its large touchhole, a flintlock

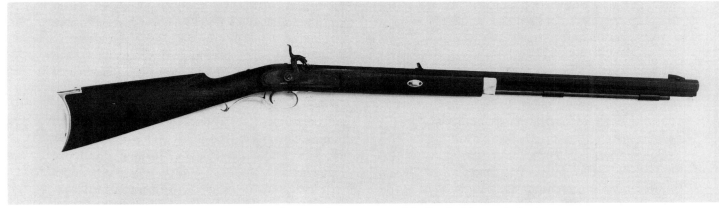

.54-caliber percussion-style trade gun. These were used by Rocky Mountain fur trappers. —Lyman

could be primed by slapping its butt to jar some of the powder charge out of the barrel and into the flash pan.

Once an Indian obtained his own gun, he usually set about modifying and decorating it. Some shortened the barrels to carbine length. Frequently, they removed the butt plates to use as scrapers. Brass-headed tacks or rawhide wrappings often adorned the wooden parts, sometimes serving dual purposes of decorating and mending broken stocks.

Although trade guns were most popular, all sorts of arms found their way into Indian hands through trade, gift, capture, or theft—army muskets and carbines, rifles, repeaters such as the Spencer, Henry, and Winchester, pistols, and revolvers. But these were in the minority; trade guns remained by far the most common firearm. And

Brown Bess flintlock muskets like this one inspired the design for Indian trade guns. —Navy Arms

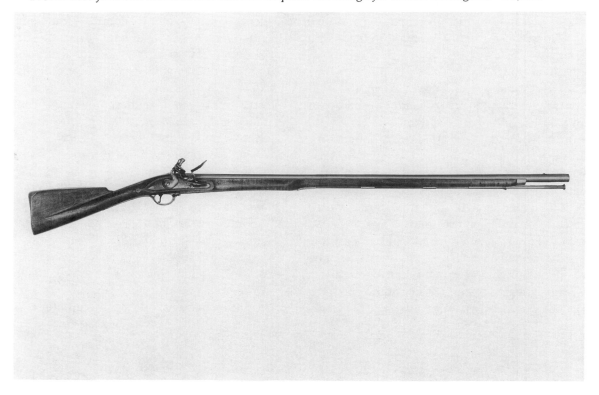

even in the late 1800s, bows and arrows were still widely used.

Another myth worth debunking is that Indians frequently were better armed than federal troops in the 1870s and 1880s. While this may have been true in a few minor encounters, soldiers—even those with Custer at Little Bighorn—were far better armed in all the major battles. As a rule, western cavalrymen usually carried both a carbine and a revolver. The Springfield .45/70 carbine issued to the troops was an accurate and dependable gun with good ballistic qualities; both the Colt single-action and the Smith & Wesson were excellent revolvers.

Indians seldom had half the number of their enemy's firearms, and most of those would have been muzzleloading smoothbores probably in poor condition; breechloaders and repeaters were rare. Of the eighty-one soldiers killed during the Fetterman Massacre in what is now Wyoming on December 21, 1866, for example, only six suffered gunshot wounds. In Custer's rout, perhaps 25-30 percent of Indians carried breechloaders and repeaters, another 25 percent had flintlocks, and the remainder only bows and arrows. All the soldiers had good firearms, grossly outnumbered though they were.

There is no basis for the stereotypical images of Indians either as dupes of greedy traders who inveigled them into struggling through the woods with seven-foot muskets or as a splendid, light cavalry, armed to the teeth with the latest repeating rifles. If an Indian had a gun at all, it probably was a lightweight flintlock smoothbore, studded with brass-headed tacks and wrapped with rawhide, its barrel rusty, and its general condition such that the average gunsmith would declare it unserviceable. And this was true from colonial times to the "winning" of the West.

Part II
A Black-Powder Primer

Chapter 4

Your First Black Powder Gun

With such a variety of black-powder guns available these days, it's easy to become a little bewildered as you try to decide which model or models best fit your needs. Before "jumping the gun" and buying the first muzzleloader you see, think about how much you want to spend, what you plan to use your weapon for, whether a flintlock or a percussion arm will serve your purposes best, and what types of sights, triggers, barrel diameters, and overall styles you should consider.

Do you want a gun for hunting? Plinking? Rendezvous or living-history reenactments? Serious competition? No single black-powder gun will fill every need or purpose. But by carefully checking out the market before you buy, you can easily acquire a front-loading gun that may serve several purposes very nicely.

If hunting is your goal, your only limitation will be matching the size of game you're after with the minimum-sized bore allowed in your state. State regulations also dictate whether you can use a muzzleloading handgun for hunting. For more information about hunting with muzzleloaders, see Appendix C. Any type and caliber of muzzleloader will work well for plinking. If you plan to participate in mountain men rendezvous or living-history reenactments of the Civil War or Revolutionary War, you will need a muzzleloader true to the appropriate historical era.

Pistols

Handguns have been around in one form or another since the very invention of firearms. In fact, the very first muzzleloading gun might have been more handgun than shoulder arm. Paintings and sketches dating from the fourteenth century clearly depict soldiers armed with a small tube-like hand cannon, held at arm's length with one hand while the other ignited it by touching a rope match to its priming charge. Over the more than six hundred years since that time, handguns and their firing systems have gone through many changes; early mechanisms included matchlocks, wheel-locks, and various flintlocks before percussion technology evolved.

Although the modes of ignition changed radically over this period, the principles of loading single-shot pistols remained basically the same. Until the introduction of percussion revolvers in the late 1830s, muzzleloading handguns were just that—loaded through the muzzle. When those newfangled cap-and-ball "revolvers" appeared, though they still relied on measured charges of black powder, they loaded from behing the barrel and offered quick, successive shots. With each cock of the hammer, the chamber revolved to align an unfired round with the bore, eliminating the need to reload until all the rounds, usually six, had been fired. Once the design became refined, shooters all but forgot about single-shot pistols.

Rifles

Thanks largely to the promotion of rifled musket competition by such organizations as the North/South Skirmish Association, interest in shooting the Civil War-era weapons is strong today. As a tribute to the 1860's craftsmen who prolifically turned out these rifled muskets, many of the original guns remain in excellent shooting condition. Demand for these guns by antique dealers, however, has driven the price of operable Models 1861, 1863, or Enfield rifled muskets sky high—well out of reach of the average black-powder shooter.

Fortunately, most of the popular models used during the Civil War are currently available as reproductions. Navy Arms, Dixie Gun Works, Euroarms of America, and a few other makers market a good selection of the big rifled muskets, many of which are actually superior to the guns produced during the Civil War years. Some of these guns are near-duplicates of the originals, while others have been modified for greater safety and reliability or to facilitate their manufacture.

Modern copies of the Remington Zouave have outsold all imported models of muzzleloading long guns. Almost every importer of guns from Italy has at one time or another offered a copy of the Zouave, only about 10,000 of which were actually used in the Civil War. At least fifty times that many of the colorful brass-mounted rifled muskets have been sold since the first ones appeared on the market during the early 1960s. Although a number of other .58-caliber rifled musket reproductions have been introduced since, the Zouave with its 33-inch barrel remains the best-selling arm of its type.

Other popular reproductions include the U.S. Model 1863 Springfield musket, the Colt 1861 Special, and the entire percussion Enfield line. Today's Civil War buffs can even own authentically detailed copies of the Confederate Cook & Brother artillery carbine and the J.P. Murry cavalry carbine. Although barrel length, stock configuration, finish, and other details can vary from one manufacturer or importer to another, all of these reproductions are designed to shoot the hollow-based minié bullet in .58 caliber.

Just as there is a broad selection of rifled musket reproductions to choose from, so too is there a good selection of bullet designs for the big-bored military muskets. Lyman, RCBS, and Lee Precision all offer bullet molds for producing a tradi-

1863 .58-caliber Zouave. Originally built by Remington, it was recognized as the most accurate military rifle of its day.
—Connecticut Valley Arms

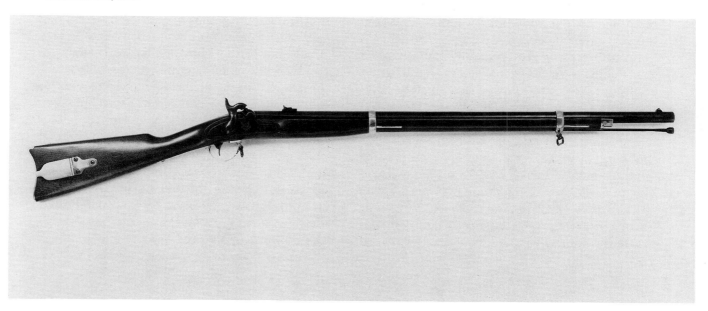

tional-styled minié with its characteristic long ogive tip and three grooves encircling the bullet. Both the RCBS and Lee bullets weigh in at 500 grains, while the old-style Lyman .58 Caliber minié weighs 460 grains. Both Lyman and Lee also offer several improved modern minié designs that greatly outperform the traditional-styled bullets in some original muskets and in practically all of the modern reproductions.

Original U.S.-made musket bores were commonly rifled at the rate of one twist in 72 inches, while the 1863 British Enfields featured one twist in 78 inches. Modern reproductions are normally rifled with one twist in 60 inches, while the rifling on the Colt 1861 Special available from Springfield Firearms Company turns once in 63 inches. Many of the Enfield copies are rifled at the rate of one turn in 48 inches. In these, the modern "improved" miniés, or the wad-cutter-styled "target" miniés available from Lee Precision, generally offer good accuracy. The Lee wad-cutter, a flat-nosed, cylindrical bullet, has no ogive-styled tip, so its entire length contacts the rifling. This design is surprisingly accurate and very popular with some North/South Skirmish shooters. The wad-cutter produces a neat, circular hole in target

paper. The improved modern minié offered by several mold makers is very similar to the Civil War-era bullets, except for its considerably shorter curve from the bullet's shank portion to its nose.

Loading Principles

Many different factors determine just how accurately a front-loading pistol or rifle can perform: the quality of steel used in its barrel, depth and twist rate of its rifling, speed and smoothness of its lock mechanisms, sureness of its ignition, and even the shooter's trigger release—all are components of accuracy. Not the least important, however, is the combination of powder, patch, and ball you load through the muzzle.

For years gun-lore writers have preached that until black-powder shooters determine some major loading formula, they may as well forget about achieving any degree of accuracy whatsoever; since each handgun or rifle is unique unto itself, the writers held, determining the perfect combination of powder, patch, and ball would be quite an accomplishment. While there's some truth to such a statement, making your new muzzleloader perform satisfactorily does not require you to know any dark secrets. In fact, all it takes is a little

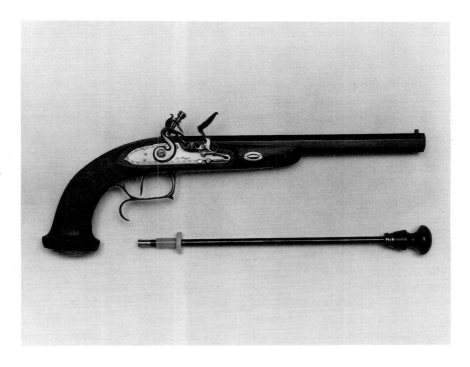

Le Page .45-caliber flintlock.
An excellent target pistol.
—*Navy Arms*

knowledge of powder granulations, patch thickness, and ball diameters—and a lot of attention to loading.

Most manufacturers or importers of muzzleloaders provide loading information with the weapons they sell. With each of its rifles, for example, Thompson/Center includes a very thorough booklet on loading, shooting, and care, along with a list of recommended loads for different calibers. Lyman and Connecticut Valley Arms provide similar data with their rifles. But not all guns come with this information, especially if you get one secondhand.

Powder Granulations. An old rule of thumb for determining a good starting load for any rifle is to match the caliber of the rifle with a like charge of black powder. Black powder comes in four grades that distinguish grain size:

Grade	Largest Grain size (inch)
Fg	.0689
FFg	.0520
FFFg	.0376
FFFFg	.0170

Use FFFg for rifles under .45 caliber and FFg for rifles over .45 caliber. Since most of today's adjustable powder flasks measure in increments of five, round up or down to the nearest mark to match your caliber of gun. For instance, if you have a .32-caliber weapon, round down the powder load to thirty grains; if your gun is .44 caliber, round up your powder charge to forty-five grains. Of course, the grains of powder to charge a .45-caliber weapon would not need to be rounded off, because you can measure an amount equal to the caliber. By following this simple rule, you can be assured of loading with neither too little nor too much powder.

Although the amount of powder you load can affect accuracy, keep in mind that its main job is only to propel the real shooting star—the bullet. Too little powder will lob the bullet in a rainbow trajectory, especially at distances over fifty yards. Too much powder could cause the bullet to strip the rifling, losing its spin and resulting in poor accuracy; worse yet, overcharging could create internal barrel pressure beyond safe limits. Usually, the most accurate target loads are those that rely on powder charges nearly equal to bore sizes. Big game hunters may end up charging their loads by as much as one-third over the rifle's caliber or bore size. Under no circumstances should you ever exceed the manufacturer's suggested maximum load for a particular model rifle!

Ball Diameters

Ball diameters seem to puzzle many beginning black-powder shooters. A variety of round balls for muzzleloading rifles are available these days; some are cast (poured from molten lead), others are swaged (fashioned from cold lead). Often different ball sizes are available for the same caliber gun: for example, either .440 or .445 (ball diameters measured in inches) can be shot from a .45-caliber rifle; similarly, .490 and .495 balls work in .50-caliber rifles. Someone just getting started might easily get confused.

Generally speaking, most modern reproduction rifles shoot accurately when loaded with a round lead ball no more than .010 of an inch smaller than the actual bore size. A .350 ball works in a .36-caliber rifle; a .530 ball works in a .54-caliber rifle, and so on. The depth of the rifling grooves determines the thickness of the patching that will yield the best results.

Patches

The majority of today's mass-produced reproduction rifles feature button rifling, with grooves commonly cut about .005-.006 inch deep in the bore. In these rifles the combination of .010-.015 inch thick patching material and a ball undersized by .010 should offer acceptable accuracy. Material heavier than .015 thick results only in a tighter fit that makes loading more difficult. However, if your rifling grooves are .010-.012 inch deep, you will need patches ranging about .015-.020; the deeper grooves require a heavier patch to fill the rifling for a sufficient gas seal.

For practical purposes, cotton cloth is the best patching available. At one time or another shooters have used linen, leather, and even canvas for patching lead balls in muzzleloading rifles. Manufacturers in the 1800s commonly supplied new rifle owners with loading and firing data: ball diameter and powder charge, along with a sample

*This recovered patch shows
perfect performance.*
—Navy Arms

of patching material and a test target fired with the rifle.

Ideal patching material has a very tight, strong weave. A patch takes a lot of abuse in the bore of a muzzleloader, where it is subjected to compression, friction, and considerable heat from the burning powder charge. A patch that tears during loading or upon ignition, or that is burnt through by the powder charge, will reduce your accuracy considerably.

Patches recovered and inspected after you shoot can tell you a lot the effectiveness of your loading combination. A patch burnt through where it came into contact with the powder charge indicates the material is too thin. If the patch is burnt through around the circumference of the ball, perhaps the patch-and-ball combination was too loose, allowing gases to blow by it in the bore. Slits in the patch might indicate a combination too tight, allowing the edges of the rifling to cut the material as you seated it and the ball with the ramrod.

A recovered patch has performed perfectly when it is blackened slightly at the rear, but not burnt through; it should have lighter streaks showing where it folded into the grooves of the rifling and a circular ring where the soft lead ball flattened slightly upon ignition to form an even tighter fit with the bore. A patch with all these indicators means you have found the correct ball-and-patch combination, and the result should be evident by the accuracy of your shot.

Lubricating your patch is important for several reasons. First, it simply makes loading easier. Lubrication helps the patch slide down the bore with less resistance, reducing the possibility of it being cut by the sharp rifling. The lube also helps the patch resist burning by the hot gases and reduces friction as it leaves the bore at high speed. Most importantly, however, the lube is vital to keeping the fouling soft from shot to shot. Fouling in a front-loading gun continues to build with each shot; the process is greatly accelerated if you do not lube your patches properly.

Many target shooters use saliva to lube their patches that will remain in the barrel for no more than a few minutes. If you are using precut patches, just pop one into your mouth as you measure the

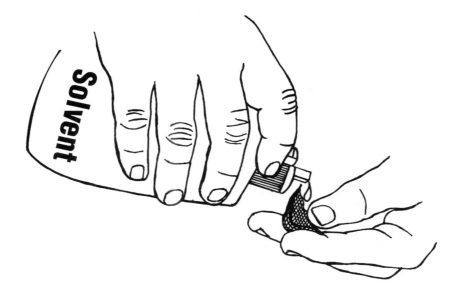

powder charge; leave it in long enough to saturate through the weave. Any lube, whether saliva or grease-based, should saturate the patch well and penetrate into the weave of the cloth. Improperly lubed patches can make a rifle impossible to load after as few as four or five shots, especially in small bores such as .32 or .36 caliber.

Precut patches are popular with modern black-powder shooters. Several suppliers offer cutters using either a hammer to punch out circular patches or a drill with circular cutting blades. Ox-Yoke Originals offers a wide selection of precut patches in a variety of diameters and cloth thicknesses for just about every muzzleloading need. Many shooters also prelube these patches by dipping them into a commercial lube or a home-brewed formula before heading out to the range or into the field.

With precut patches it's more important to make sure the patch at least encircles the circumference of the ball than it is to actually center the ball in the patch. If the patch is centered, however, the ball will be completely patched on all sides. The fact that more patching rides ahead of the ball in the bore on one side than the other

has little, if any, effect on accuracy. Muzzleloading authorities have experimented with square and triangular patches and found them comparable in accuracy to perfectly round ones.

One way to be sure that a ball is completely encircled by the patching material is to use bulk patching and cut it at the muzzle. To use patching like bulk or strips of cotton cloth or pillow tickling, place a properly lubed section of material over the muzzle and thumb a ball in as far as it will go. With the flat surface of a short starter, punch the ball and patching into the bore flush with the muzzle, then cut the excess material flush with the muzzle with a sharp patch knife.

Cleaning. Black-powder guns require a thorough cleaning after each shooting session, and, for best results, occasional quick cleanings during the session. With single-shot weapons, run a damp patch followed by a dry one through the bore after each shot to maximize your accuracy. Do the same for revolvers after firing the full cylinder.

Care and respect for your black-powder gun will enhance both your enjoyment of shooting and your gun's performance.

Chapter 5

Loading Your Weapon

Single-Shot Pistols

Although the single-shot pistol and the percussion revolver are both considered black-powder handguns, loading them differs markedly. For all practical purposes, loading a single-shot black-powder pistol is the same as loading a single-shot black-powder rifle—it takes powder, patch, and ball. Since most handguns of this sort feature barrels measuring fewer than ten inches in length, obtaining the ideal combination of powder, patch, and ball is even more critical than with most muzzleloading rifles. The short pistol barrel is a lot less forgiving than a three-foot rifle barrel. A single-shot pistol very popular with modern black-powder shooters is the Thompson/Center Patriot. Its nine-inch barrel is rifled with eight grooves twisting at the rate of one turn in twenty-two inches—three times the rate found in some front-loading rifle barrels.

When loading a percussion single-shot pistol, first snap a couple of caps on the nipple to make sure the flash channel leading from the nipple to the barrel is clear of any oil and all obstructions. If the pistol is a flintlock, look for any blockage in the vent leading from the pan to the barrel. If you see any obstruction, clear it with a small wire or quill by running it in and out of the vent several times.

Next, measure out a charge of black powder or the non-fouling propellant Pyrodex and dump it down the bore. Use straight Pyrodex only for percussion pistols. For flint pistols, drop in a few grains of black powder first to ensure ignition; Pyrodex is a little harder to ignite than the old standard black powder and the flash from a flintlock pan normally won't do the trick. Using up to five grains of FFg has little effect on the non-fouling properties of Pyrodex.

Competition shooters usually have the convenience of benches and stands to hold their pistols while they load. A loading stand simply holds the pistol's muzzle pointed skyward; some are padded to protect the finish of the stock. Shooters loading in the field generally place the butt of the handgun against their hip, holding the pistol with the trigger guard toward them and the muzzle angled slightly away.

After charging the bore, tap a percussion pistol lightly a few times to make sure that at least a few granules of powder enter the flash channel leading from the bolster or drum-and-nipple arrangement. This step can be omitted with a flint pistol since the vent hole leading from the pan opens directly to the powder charge in the barrel. If the vent hole allows some of the fine granules of powder to fall through from the barrel, block it with a feather quill or something similar to prevent powder from being blown out when you seat the ball, compressing the air between the patched ball and your powder charge.

If you use a precut patch, carefully center it over the muzzle of the barrel and push the ball into the bore as far as possible with your thumb, then

The design of this .45-caliber Patriot, an excellent target pistol, was inspired by traditional duelling models. —Thompson/Center

A .58-caliber Harpers Ferry flintlock. —Navy Arms

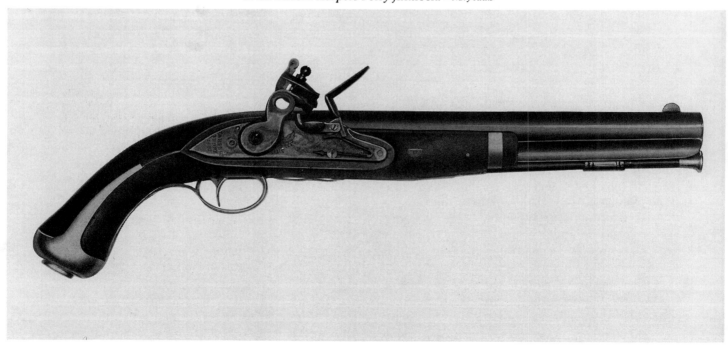

use a short starter to inch the patch and ball into the barrel. (See illustrations in the rifle section of this chapter.) If your starter rod is too short to seat the ball properly over the powder charge, use your ramrod to complete the step. Some pistol starters come with a ten- to twelve-inch auxiliary rod, which works fine for loading at a bench but is awkward to carry in the field.

When using bulk or strip patching, first lubricate the cloth in an area about the same diameter as the barrel either by smearing it with a commercial lube or by wetting it with saliva. Drape the lubed area over the muzzle, then thumb a ball into the bore. Use the starter to drive the ball and patching into the bore until they are flush with the muzzle—one good smack on the backside of the starter with the palm of your free hand usually does the trick—then trim the excess material with your patch knife. Start the patched ball down the muzzle with your short starter, then seat it with your ramrod. After seating a percussion cap over the nipple, you're gun is ready to fire.

Cap-and-Ball Revolvers

Start by cleaning out the oil and clearing the nipples as described above. After doing this, move the hammer to the half-cock position so you can turn the cylinder by hand. Drop the proper measure of powder into one chamber and place an unpatched ball over the powder at the chamber's mouth. If the gun is a Ruger Old Army .44 or another gun of that caliber, a suitable charge is twenty-five grains of FFFg black powder with a .457 round ball. Repeat the process until all the chambers are loaded, then fill the mouth of each chamber with grease to prevent multiple discharge and soften the fouling. Cap the nipples, and the gun is ready to fire.

If you plan to carry a loaded revolver in a holster, it's best to leave the chamber under the hammer completely unloaded, not just uncapped; otherwise, the fire from one percussion cap could jump into the nipple vent of your loaded but uncapped chamber, and double ignition could occur.

—Ruger

RUGER®
OLD ARMY®
Cap and Ball Revolver
.44 Caliber Black Powder

Stainless Steel
KBP-7   7½" barrel

Percussion Rifles

Before loading either a percussion or flint rifle, run a dry cleaning patch down, then up and out of the bore to remove any excess oil from the previous cleaning; use a cleaning jag attached to the end of your ramrod. If you have a percussion rifle, snap a few caps on the nipple to blow out any oil caught in the flash channel. Check for clear ignition by holding the muzzle against a blade of grass or a small leaf as you snap the caps; air pressure from the caps should cause the leaf to flutter slightly, assuring you the channel is clear. Once you have determined the channel leading from the nipple to the barrel is clear of any obstruction, half cock the rifle's hammer, then measure a charge from your powder horn or flask and dump it into the muzzle, holding the muzzle angled slightly away from your body.

Never charge a muzzleloader directly from any sort of powder reservoir, no matter how completely the reservoir may be cut off from the charger-dispenser. With a quarter to a half pound of powder inside, the reservoir is a potential bomb! A tiny ember left burning in the bore could ignite the works right under your face. Keep muzzleloading safe. Always use a separate measure.

After dumping the measured powder into the bore, make sure that some of the granules find their way into the narrow flash channel by lightly tapping the side of the rifle a few times. Patch a ball of the proper diameter and start it into the bore of the rifle, either using a precut patch or trimming the patching at the muzzle. Remember, the muzzle of the rifle should always be angled away from you.

Many shooters rely on a short starter to get the patched ball four or five inches into the bore before using the ramrod to finish seating the ball over the powder charge. You have to concentrate on what you're doing at all times when loading a muzzleloader. Don't forget to finish seating the ball over the powder charge or you'll shoot a short-started ball. Light target loads in a good quality barrel may have little effect on your barrel if you fire a short-started ball. But heavier charges, such as those used in hunting, could make the short-started ball act like a barrel obstruction and result in a bulged or blown barrel. For this reason, many

.54-caliber Great Plains reproduction rifle, a model made famous by fur trappers of the Rocky Mountains.
—Lyman

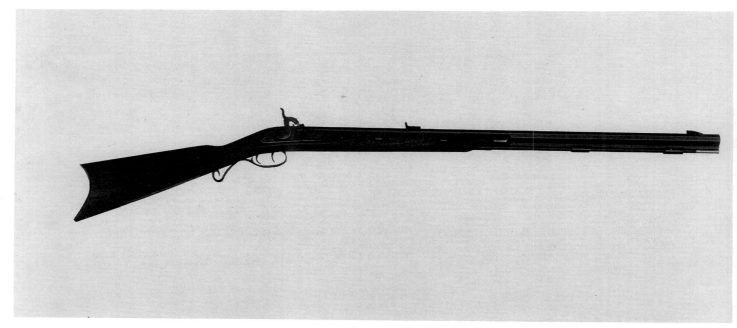

Loading a Percussion or Flint Rifle

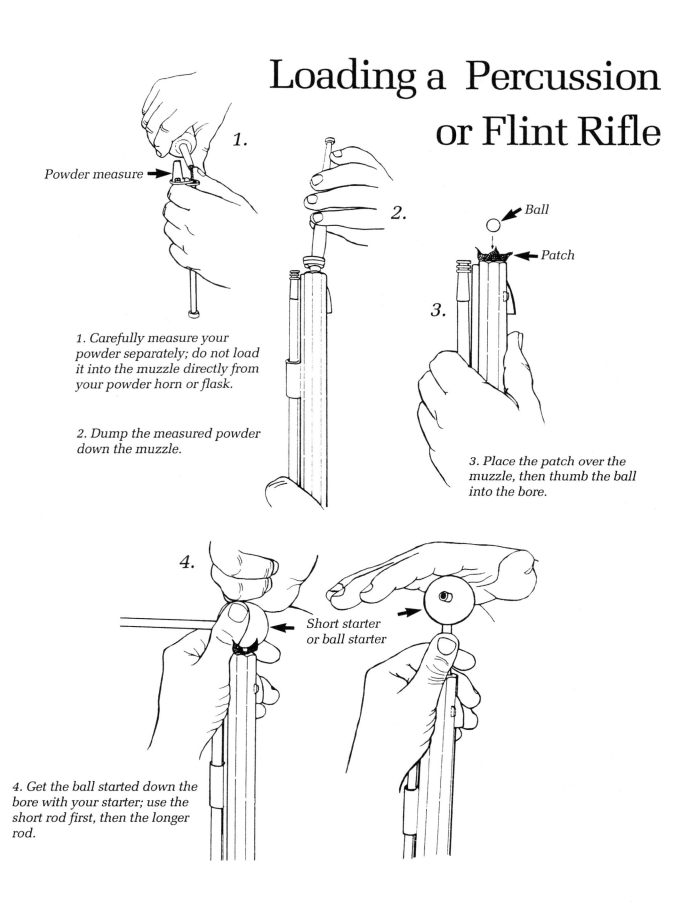

Powder measure →

1. →

Ball

Patch

2.

3.

1. Carefully measure your powder separately; do not load it into the muzzle directly from your powder horn or flask.

2. Dump the measured powder down the muzzle.

3. Place the patch over the muzzle, then thumb the ball into the bore.

4.

Short starter or ball starter

4. Get the ball started down the bore with your starter; use the short rod first, then the longer rod.

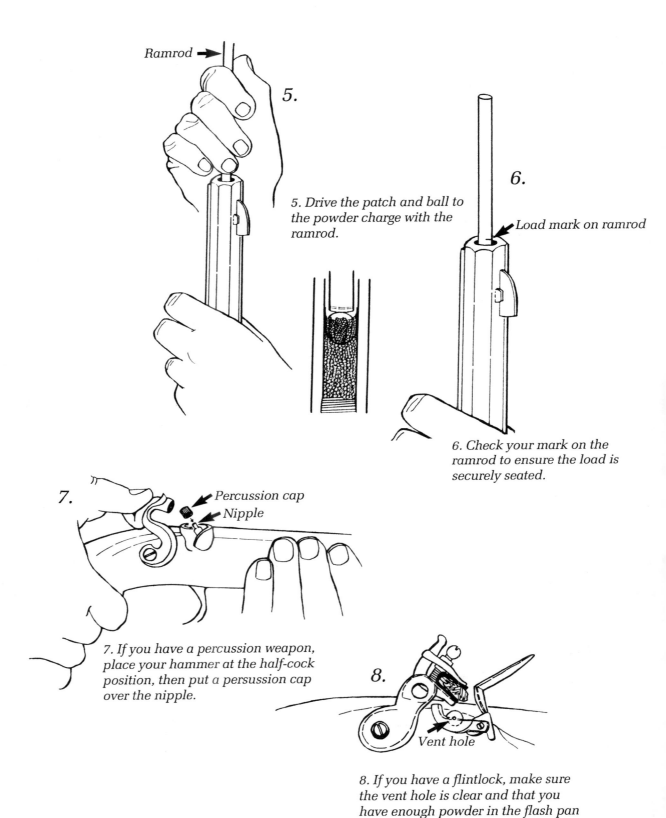

Ramrod →

5.

5. Drive the patch and ball to the powder charge with the ramrod.

6.

← Load mark on ramrod

6. Check your mark on the ramrod to ensure the load is securely seated.

7.

Percussion cap
Nipple

7. If you have a percussion weapon, place your hammer at the half-cock position, then put a persussion cap over the nipple.

8.

Vent hole

8. If you have a flintlock, make sure the vent hole is clear and that you have enough powder in the flash pan to ensure ignition.

target shooters no longer use starters; instead, they seat the ball all the way from the muzzle to its position over the powder charge using the ramrod. If the patch-and-ball combination is well-suited to the rifle, resistance is light.

It's best to mark your ramrod in some way to indicate when the ball is all the way down the barrel and firmly on top of the powder charge. When your barrel starts to build up fouling, seating the ball can become increasingly difficult; fouling build-up can fool you into thinking that the ball is all the way down when it's not. By marking your ramrod you will know for sure when the ball is properly seated on top of the powder charge. When seating the ball with the ramrod, never place your hands or face over the end of the rod—a lingering ember from your previous shot could cause your rifle to fire prematurely.

After loading your rifle, place a percussion cap on the nipple to arm it. When shooting at a range where others are present, wait until you are on the firing line before capping your rifle. At all times, remember to keep the muzzle pointed in a safe direction and the hammer at half cock. When bringing a percussion rifle to full cock, never release the spur of the hammer until you're sure the sear crisply and positively engages the full cock notch of the tumbler, otherwise the gun may fire when you release the hammer.

Flintlock Rifles

Loading a flintlock rifle is very similar to loading a percussion rifle. The first step is to make sure the flash hole leading from the pan to bore is clear; use a vent pick to do this. Then drop the hammer all the way down, so the flint is facing into the open pan with the frizzen (actually, "frizzle," or strike plate, but commonly called "frizzen") all the way open. For absolute safety, it's even a good idea to slip a leather cover over the frizzen to prevent accidental spark. If the vent hole is large enough, stick the quill of a small feather into the flash hole to prevent fine powder granules from being blown back through the vent hole as you ram the patched ball down over the powder charge, compressing the air in the bore.

Once the ball is firmly seated on the powder, remove the quill and charge the pan with a few grains of super-fine FFFFg black powder. Don't heap the powder—just half a pan will generally result in better ignition than a full pan. It's the flash that actually fires the powder charge inside the bore, not the burning granules themselves. Always keep a close watch on the edge of the flint to see that the priming powder has not fouled the face of the frizzen. It takes a really good shower of sparks to ensure ignition every time with a flintlock.

Wait until you're on the firing line at the shooting range before charging the pan of your flint rifle. When hunting, flip the frizzle shut over the primed pan and carry the hammer at half-cock; even this precaution cannot guarantee that your rifle will not accidently discharge, so keep the muzzle pointed in a safe direction at all times. When shooting either a flint or percussion rifle, wipe fouling from the bore after every fourth or fifth shot to maintain accuracy. If you are at a shooting range, where a loading bench is handy, you can use one of the auxiliary stainless steel loading rods to save your rifle's wooden ramrod for field use. These stainless steel rods have Teflon™ or nylon muzzle protectors that eliminate ramrod wear on the rifling at the muzzle and are a lot tougher than the hickory rods most front-loading rifles come with, especially the slender 5/16-inch diameter rods required for most .32- and .36-caliber rifles.

You can quickly clear fouling from your bore by attaching a cleaning jag to your ramrod and running a cleaning patch lightly dampened with saliva or a commercial solvent-lube—like Birchwood Casey No. 77 black-powder solvent—through it. The idea is not to scrub the bore spotless, but just to eliminate fouling build-up. If you over-saturate the cleaning patch, you might need a second dry patch to remove excess moisture from the barrel. Once wiped, the barrel will load as easily as it did at the beginning of your shooting session.

The suggested patch-and-ball combinations, powder charges, and loading procedures given here might or might not produce the absolute best performance from your rifle; but they will offer you acceptable beginning accuracy. Obtaining top performance from a rifle might require many shots to refine your load measurements and properly align your sights. Seldom do shooters find a single load suitable for everything from targets to big game. Many shooters develop two or even three different loads for the same rifle: for example, a light powder charge and tight patch-and-ball combination for target practice, and a fairly heavy powder charge and easier-loading patch-and-ball combination for hunting and field use. Some even rely on slightly different powder charges for shooting at different ranges: for example, a light forty-grain charge for targets at twenty-five yards; fifty grains at fifty yards; and maybe as much as sixty or seventy grains at a hundred yards. Such varying charges allow you to maintain the same sight alignment on targets at different distances.

Hawken flintlock outfit. —Thompson/Center

MAXI-BALLS

| .36 CAL. | .45 CAL. | .50 CAL. | .54 CAL. |
| 128 GRS. | 220 GRS. | 370 GRS. | 400 GRS. |

—*Thompson/Center*

Although patched round balls are fairly well established as traditional bullets for muzzleloading rifles, many modern muzzleloading hunters have switched to one of several hard-hitting, maximum-performance conical bullet designs for the added knockdown power they offer on big game. These don't require a patch of any sort, relying instead on one or more slightly oversized bearing bands and obturation (flattening) of the bullet in the bore upon ignition for a precision fit with the rifling. For that reason, bullets such as the Thompson/Center Maxi-Ball and the Lee Precision R.E.A.L. (rifling engraved at loading) bullet perform best in bores that have rather shallow (.005-.006) button grooves. When used in deeper-grooved (.010-.012) bores, these bullets run the risk of not flattening sufficiently to seal the grooves, resulting in gas blow-by and poor accuracy.

The safest, best-built, and most accurate muzzleloading rifles ever made are the modern reproductions. It doesn't take a $1,000 custom rifle with a custom-cut barrel to produce target-quality accuracy. Many major shooting matches across the country are won annually by people shooting mass-produced reproduction rifles that cost $200-$300. Surely expensive, custom-made rifles offer serious competitors an edge, but shooters who spend that much money and time on such rifles likely pay lots of attention to how and with what they load them.

Once you find the proper combination of powder, patch, and ball for your rifle—whether it's a top-of-the-line custom job or a reproduction muzzleloader—always load it with your proven formula. Any deviation from this combination is sure to affect your accuracy. Every load in a muzzleloader's barrel is akin to a custom-reloaded cartridge for a modern arm. The care and attention you take during loading will result in more accurate shooting, and hitting what you're aiming at adds a whole lot to the enjoyment of shooting a muzzleloading rifle.

These thoughts would not be complete without a few words about shooting safety. For what should be obvious reasons, wear a good pair of shooting glasses to prevent serious eye injury. Left-handed shooters should not use flintlock black-powder long guns with the hammer on the right side of the lock. If they do, they will find all the ignition action taking place right in their faces—not a pleasant experience. If you're left-handed, shoot only a left-handed version of a percussion gun, whether it is from a kit, factory-finished, or a custom job.

CHAPTER 6

ACCESSORIES

The Essentials

The basic necessities for loading and shooting a muzzleloading firearm are really quite simple—propellent, projectile, and fire for the ignition. The propellent can either be black powder or Pyrodex, a modern substitute. The projectile may be a traditional patched round ball or one of the newer conical bullets, such as the Thompson/Center Maxi-Ball. Fire for the ignition comes from either the sharpened edge of a knapped flint striking the hardened steel surface of a frizzen, igniting a few grains of FFFFg in the flash pan or, if you have a percussion rifle, a percussion cap placed on the nipple. And that's all that's really needed to make a front-loading rifle functional.

So why is it that when black powder-shooters head for the range or out for an afternoon of plinking, they burden themselves with shooting pouches or boxes loaded with all sorts of accessories for their rifles? Muzzleloading is one of those sports that seems to have no limit when it comes to accessories. Sure, you can get by with just the basics, but the luxury afforded by adding various accessories makes muzzleloading much more enjoyable. Also, some of these so-called accessories are so important during loading that they should be considered essentials.

Powder Measures

A powder measure is one of the most important accessories. Top performance from any front-loading gun—be it a rifle, pistol, revolver, musket, or scattergun—depends on consistent powder charges. Most commercially available measures allow you to adjust your powder charges in graduated increments of five or ten grains; these work well but aren't all that necessary. Any type of measure—even a cutoff center-fire cartridge case or hollowed out wooden tube or section of deer antler—permits you to load with a consistent amount of powder.

An adjustable measure is handy if you use different powder charges for different ranges, if you are experimenting with loads, or if you shoot more than one black powder gun. Navy Arms makes a measure with settings from 10 to 120 grains, marked in ten-grain increments. Any setting can be locked into place by tightening a knurled nut on the side of the measure, which

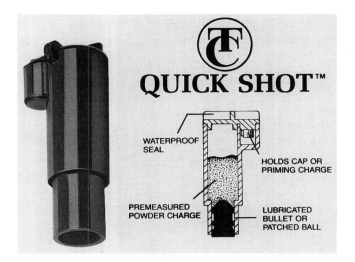

Quick Shot™, a tempting accessory. —Thompson/Center

keeps all charges identical until you change the setting. Its funnel top swivels to one side for easy filling, then swivels back over the top of the measure to level the powder charge and provide a pour spout that gets every granule of powder into the bore. The bottom of this measure unscrews to reveal a stiff, small-diameter wire that works well to clear nipples or vents.

Thompson/Center also offers a well-built, adjustable brass powder measure. This one adjusts from 20 to 120 grains, with a locking, knurled collet to retain the desired setting until you want to readjust it to a new setting. Instead of a swiveling funnel head, the head on this one slips back and forth. To fill the measure, push the funnel out of the way to one side, then fill the measure and

push the funnel back over the powder charge. The powder charge levels automatically, allowing you to easily pour the charge into the muzzle of your gun. In the measure's base is a compartment for caps, which holds about twenty standard No. 11 percussion caps.

Dixie Gun Works offers a small adjustable measure very similar to the Navy Arms model described above. Like the larger measure, this one also features a funnel-type head that swivels out of the way for easy filling. The Dixie measures only 5 to 40 grains, however, in five-grain increments. The small measure is less than half the size of its Navy Arms counterpart, making it ideal to use with a small-bore rifle or pistol that normally loads with fewer than forty grains of powder.

Powder Horns

From the beginning, black-powder shooters have struggled with how to carry a readily available supply of powder for reloading. They've tried bags made of waterproofed goatskin; flasks fashioned from hollowed-out red stag antlers were once popular in Germany; and some Spanish conquistadors armed with matchlocks carried premeasured charges in wooden tubes arranged in bandoleer fashion. North American shooters have traditionally relied either on horns from cattle or metal powder flasks.

Powder horns come in all sizes and shapes and with nearly every imaginable embellishment. Although the common horn carried by frontiersmen in the late 1700s and early 1800s was nearly always left plain, except for perhaps the owner's name or initials, some real pieces of art also came from that period. Usually either the owner or someone specializing in custom powder horns carved and scrimshawed elaborate designs into the bony exterior. Some fine old original powder horns have maps of entire regions etched into their surfaces, and, surprisingly, some of them are extremely accurate for maps drawn without the aid of modern instruments.

When selecting a powder horn, look for several features. First, it should not be too large. Horns offered by some the dealers and mail-order firms are large enough to carry a pound or more of powder; this is not necessary. Unless you find one that is exceptionally thick, a powder horn measuring about ten to twelve inches in length and about eight inches in circumference at its base should hold about half a pound of powder—more than enough to get you through a match. A smaller horn holding about one-third pound of powder will provide you enough propellent for just about any hunting trip.

Always inspect the horn's base plug carefully to make sure it is reasonably watertight. Any moisture seepage here could result in damp powder that not only resists ignition, but, if it becomes too wet, could break down and nearly dissolve. If wet powder dries out inside the horn, it could become a solid chunk that will never come out of the pour spout. Some commercially produced powder horns feature a base plug with a center portion that unscrews for easy filling. Although this is a nice feature, never sacrifice moisture protection for ease of filling. Remember your priorities.

If the horn you're considering is fitted with a stopper-like arrangement to close off its pour spout, make sure the stopper fits securely and can't easily be jarred from the opening. Many horns are fitted with a spring-loaded valve threaded to accept a variety of spouts. Several firms offer these spouts for different charge weights, making it inviting to load directly from the powder horn instead of relying on a powder measure. This is dangerous. Even the slightest burning ember left in the bore could ignite the fresh charge of powder as you pour it through the muzzle. Although the spring-loaded valves do a remarkably good job of sealing off the powder inside the horn, direct charging is not worth the risk. A half-pound of powder igniting all at once is powerful enough to maim.

Molding block for Maxi-hunter bullets.
—*Thompson/Center*

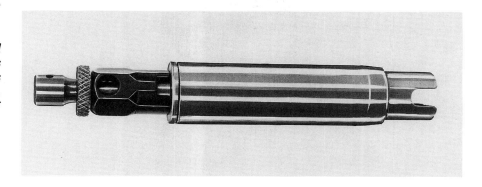

This six-in-one combo tool services nipples, stores caps, and measures black powder.
—Thompson/Center

Powder flasks come in all sizes and shapes. Tiny flasks that fit inside a cased pistol set run only about four and a half inches in length and will hold only 400-500 grains of powder. Others, like the eight-inch long Zouave rifle flask, hold just over a half pound of powder. One of the most popular flasks is a copy of the one that originally accompanied the Colt percussion Model 1851 Navy revolver. This flask measures right at six inches long and holds slightly more than one-third pound of powder.

Practically all powder flasks are made of either brass or copper. Usually a spring-loaded lever operated manually opens and closes an internal valve that regulates the flow of powder from the flask. Dixie Gun Works offers a cylindrical powder flask made of extra-heavy brass capable of supporting the weight of an average man without denting. Either end unscrews for easy filling, and one end is fitted with a button-operated, spring-loaded valve threaded to accept a spout, while the other end is fitted with a lanyard ring. Various sizes of spouts can be threaded into most flasks, again, encouraging shooters to engage in the unsafe practice of charging their guns directly from the flask instead of using a separate measure. The metal bodies of most powder flasks make them potentially more dangerous than the powder horn.

Ball Starters

Another important accessory is a ball starter, especially if you use bulk patching material. Most starters have a short quarter-inch stub and a four-to-six-inch section of rod. The body of the starter may be a wooden ball or a heavy piece of deer antler or even polyurethane casting resin.

When using the ball starter with bulk patching material, press the patched ball into the bore as far as it will go with your thumb. Using the short part of your starter, push the cloth-and-lead wad to just below the muzzle's crown. Trim the excess cloth with a sharp knife, then, with the longer starter rod, push the patched ball far enough into the bore to permit insertion of the ramrod, with which you'll seat the ball over the powder charge.

With precut patches you probably won't need to use the short section of the starter. Instead, center the ball in the patch with the patch centered over the bore, then use the longer starter rod and a healthy shove get both patch and ball well into the bore. Some elongated conical bullets rely on oversized bearing bands for a precise fit with the bore. Getting the rifling to engage these bands often requires a considerable amount of pressure on the bullet's nose. The use of a short starter helps to get these bullets started by pushing them into the bore four or five inches, at which point the rifling has fully engraved any oversized portions of the bullet.

Pocket packs, lube, short starter, powder measure, nipple wrench, and spare nipple. —Thompson/Center

Most mail-order muzzleloading suppliers sell a short or ball starter. Most are simply a one-and-a-half- to two-inch diameter wooden ball with two rod sections set into it. The rods are commonly made of hardwood dowels, but occasionally brass or special non-abrasive plastic is used. Some competition shooters rely on a short steel starter with a nylon bushing that protects the rifling at the muzzle from wear.

Patches

The convenience of loading with precut patching, such as that offered by Ox-Yoke Originals, has caused a large percentage of today's shooters to stray from loading with bulk patching. However, it's not always possible to purchase patches in the thickness you need or of a diameter suitable for muzzleloading rifles or pistols. For emergency use, it's best to have a yard or so of bulk patching material that you can use, even if temporarily, until you can get a new batch of precut patches. When you load with bulk patching or patching strips, you'll need a patch knife of some sort to trim away the excess material.

Just about any sharp knife will work to cut patching. The old Russell Green River line of knives includes several that make fine patch knives. One knife comes with rounded end for safety. The two-and-a-half-inch blade is plenty long for trimming away patch material; you could attach a lanyard to help prevent losing the knife if you carry it in a scabbard attached to the shooting patch strap. Another superb Green River patch knife is actually cataloged as a Pacific paring knife. Its three-inch blade has an almost-square tip and looks a lot like an old straight razor. Straight razors also make great patch knives because they quickly fold into the handle for safe and convenient storage inside your shooting bag.

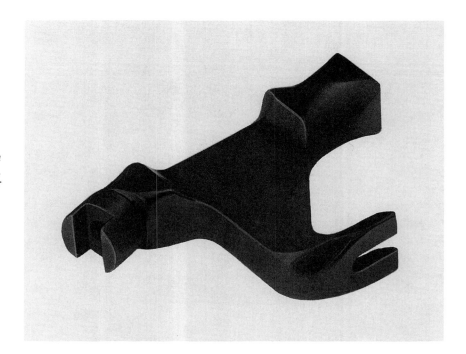

Combination wedge-pin puller and nipple wrench.
—*Thompson/Center*

Cappers

Although not necessarily an accessory, a capper can make loading a percussion gun a little less tedious. Most muzzleloading supply firms either import or produce an in-line capper that, as the name implies, holds a line of caps inside a slender, rectangular body. One end is closed; the other is fitted with a pair of spring-steel fingers. Internally, most straight-line cappers utilize a coil spring and a sliding stop. To fill one of these, pull back the stop past a hole in the capper and drop the caps in one at a time, cup side down. When the capper is full (most hold about twenty caps), release the sliding stop, which pushes the caps toward the open end. The stop doesn't always put tension on the caps, but it keeps them from getting back to the opening through which they were loaded.

To use a straight-line capper, push on the sliding stop to advance a cap into the grasp of the spring-steel fingers. These hold the cap until you slip it over the cone of the nipple. When you pull the capper rearward away from the nipple, the cap

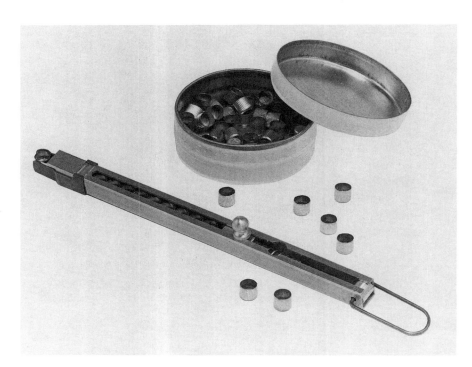

In-line straight capper and tin of #11 percussion caps.
—*Thompson/Center*

will easily separate from the spring-steel fingers. Cappers designed like this work well with rifles, pistols, and revolvers requiring standard No.11 percussion caps.

Another popular capper is the oval style available from Cash Manufacturing—an exact copy of the oval rifle cappers popular with black-powder shooters in the mid to late 1800s. The modern version generously holds seventy-five No. 11 caps, and its entire top swings upward for easy filling. You can shake the caps into an upright position by vibrating the capper slightly; the heavier, enclosed ends will roll over after just a few seconds until all of the caps rest upright. To use the Cash capper, hold the small opening of the slightly pointed end downward and push the small button on the side in with your thumb. This operates an inside lever that allows a cap to drop down into the opening. Releasing the button causes the lever to put pressure against the cap from one side and against a thin piece of spring steel on the other side, holding the cap securely in the opening until you slip the cupped portion over the cone of a nipple. Pulling the capper rearward easily disengages the cap from the grasp of the lever and spring. This is one of the handiest and most trouble-free capper designs ever devised.

White Mountain .50-caliber carbine outfit. —Thompson/Center

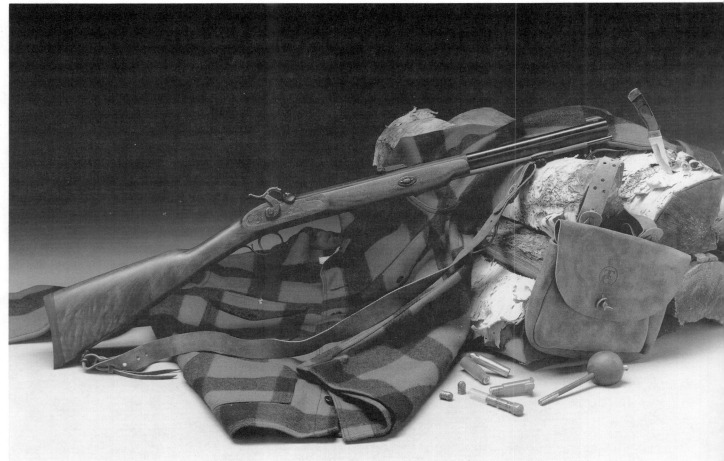

Shooting Bags

To carry all this gear, you need a good shooting bag, or "possibles" bag, as some prefer to call it. Better designs always have several internal pockets or compartments. The partitions help keep all your gear separated and easy to find when you need something. Although powder horns or flasks are normally carried outside the shooting bag, you can carry quite a bit of loading paraphernalia inside.

Many shooters seem to go overboard when selecting a bag, shopping for the biggest their money can buy. The trouble is, larger bags allow you to stuff perhaps too much inside them. Before deciding on a shooting bag, think about what you need to carry in it. An uncrowded bag allows you to find what you want when you want it. Powder measure, balls, capper, pan primer for a flint gun, patching, ball starter and maybe a patch knife are your basic loading accessories. Anything else will just complicate your loading process.

Once you have acquired the basic accessories that make loading easier and more convenient, not to mention more consistent, you can start shopping around for those additional little luxury items that make the sport a little more pleasant. These include a small knapping hammer to keep the striking edge of your flint nice and sharp or a nipple wrench if you have a percussion gun, a loading block for faster reloading in the field, a patch cutter for precutting patches at home, a screw-in funnel for spill-free filling of your powder horn or flask, a specially adapted nipple and cover to make your percussion rifle virtually waterproof, a set of sling swivels or a slip-on sling, a mechanical starter for Maxi-Balls, a stainless steel combination loading-cleaning rod, an internal safety for the Thompson/Center rifle, or perhaps even a shooting box to carry some of these items out to the range.

Part III
Hunting with Muzzleloaders

CHAPTER 7

BIG GAME

Rifles

Hunting big game with muzzleloaders has finally come back into its own in recent years. Every state in the U.S. allows hunters to use of one type of muzzleloader or another during the regular firearms big game season. Many states hold separate muzzleloading-only, black powder-only, or primitive weapons hunts; some even allow hunters to tag additional game. This chapter evaluates some of the more popular muzzleloading rifle styles, hunting projectiles, the powder charges needed to turn a front-loading long gun into a potent big game rifle, and the role of sidearms in hunting big game.

Without a doubt deer are the number one big game animals hunted today in the United States. They also are the target of choice by the current crop of black-powder hunters. In some parts of the country, hunting for deer with front-loading weapons has become so popular that the number of muzzleloading permits issued annually by state game departments exceeds archery permits. Nearly 45,000 hunters annually take part in Arkansas's muzzleloader deer hunt, with almost as many black-powder shooters hunting in neighboring Mississippi. Pennsylvania, a state renowned for its exceptional deer hunting, has drawn as many as 140,000 hunters for its weeklong flintlock muzzleloading season. Though hunters get more time in the field, they are not allowed to harvest additional deer.

Unless state regulations dictate otherwise, today's muzzleloading hunters tend to favor as practical a front-loading rifle as they can find. This normally means a rifle with a short barrel for faster handling. Rifles with barrels between twenty-six and thrity-two inches have been the best sellers. Black-powder shooters more interested in the harvest than in using traditional equipment also strongly favor a rear sight fully adjustable for windage and elevation.

When Turner Kirkland first introduced his Dixie Kentucky rifle back in the mid-1950s, it was available in .40 caliber only, following the tradition of many original rifles. By the early 1960s, however, many shooters wanted to try their hands at hunting deer with a black-powder front-loader, but felt the .40-caliber Dixie rifle was not up to the job. To meet the demand for a slightly larger and more effective deer rifle, Dixie upped the caliber to .45. These larger rifles reigned in popularity through the 1960s and into the early 1970s. The larger caliber allowed shooters to load up with more powder for taking deer and other big game and load down for smaller game.

As more and more states began to allow the use of muzzleloaders for big game hunting and started to implement muzzleloading-only hunts, increasing numbers of hunters took to black powder. In the early 1970s .50-caliber rifles began overtaking .45s in popularity. Most hunters found the .45-

caliber rifles, especially when loaded with a patched round ball, ineffective for deer-sized game. The increased weight of 178-grain balls used in the .50-caliber rifles over the 128-grain balls normally fired in the .45s often meant the difference between putting a deer down quickly versus having to make a long and difficult search for a wounded animal.

Most deer are taken as close as fifty yards or less; at that range, the patched round ball is ideal. The soft lead sphere retains enough of the velocity and energy it had at the muzzle to drive home with quite a wallop. Driven by 70-90 grains of FFg or FFFg, a patched 178-grain .490 ball generally will not punch all the way through the body of a grown deer at fifty yards. A ball that completely stops inside the body transfers all its energy to the animal for a clean kill; one that passes completely through the body wastes some of its energy. It is not uncommon for a .490-diameter ball to flatten into a disk nearly half again its original diameter.

For shots at forty to sixty yards, the patched round ball is actually a much better choice of projectile than a solid-based or hollow-based cy-

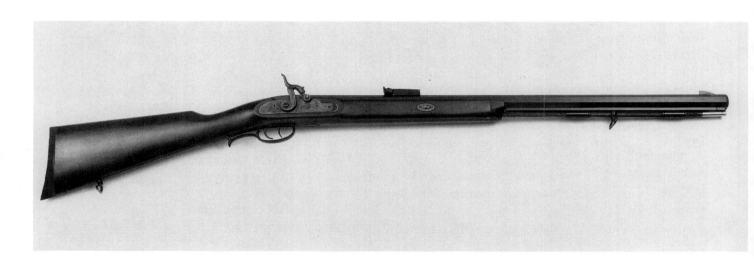

A well-matched set: the Hunter Hawken rifle (above) and Hawken pistol (below) are both .50-caliber percussion weapons. The rifle is a good choice for deer sized game. —Connecticut Valley Arms

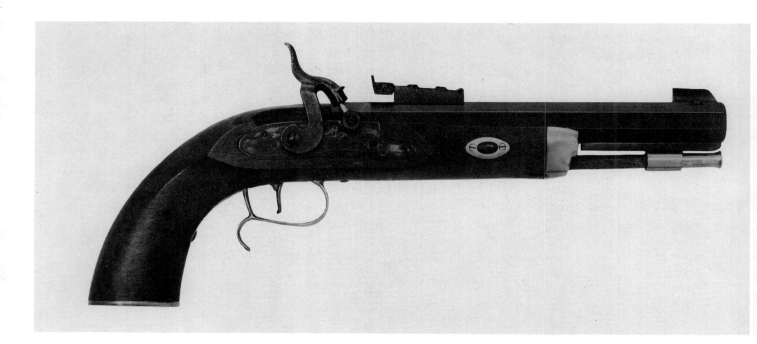

lindrical bullet, like the Thompson/Center Maxi-Ball or one of the minié-type bullets. These gray hunks of lead certainly drive home with more wallop. But on closer targets they develop too much energy; their added weight tends to push right through the body of a deer at less than forty yards. For shots of seventy-five to one hundred yards, the Maxi-Balls are a better choice than the patched round ball, which begin losing velocity and energy at that distance. The patched ball at a hundred yards has little more than one-third the velocity and energy it had at the muzzle. In some cases, this might not be enough to ensure a clean kill.

A .50-caliber rifle with a 32-inch barrel, loaded with ninety grains of FFFg behind a patched .490-diameter ball will produce a muzzle velocity of about 1,890 feet per second (fps) and release 1,425 foot-pounds of muzzle energy upon firing. At one hundred yards the ball will slow to barely over 700 fps and hit the target with only about 465 pounds of energy—hardly potent deer load. A Thompson/Center 370-grain Maxi-Ball from the same muzzle leaves at about 1,470 fps and maintains around 1,765 foot-pounds of muzzle energy—more than enough for dropping a hefty buck.

The Thompson/Center Maxi-Ball can turn a borderline .45-caliber into a very potent big game rifle shooting at distances of fifty to seventy-five yards. Most .45-caliber rifles rely on a 128-grain .440 round ball. The Maxi-Ball for a .45 weighs 240 grains, nearly double the weight of the round ball. Similarly, the 370-grain .50-caliber and 430-grain .54-caliber Maxi-Balls are approximately double the weight of round balls fired in the same caliber rifles. Being heavier, however, the big conical bullets require more powder to get them rolling along. Powder charges of around a hundred grains are fairly common, even in .50-caliber rifles.

Experienced hunters almost always have a good idea at what range they are likely to shoot from, enabling them to load up with appropriate powder charges and bullets in advance. This is especially true if they hunt year after year from a familiar stand. When hunting in unfamiliar country, it's better to be slightly overgunned than to pack a rifle that might not have the power for dropping a deer at the outermost effective limits of a front-loading rifle. Shooting one of the big Maxi-type bullets at close range is preferable to taking a long shot with a patched round ball. There is no substitute for good shot placement, no matter what the projectile. Even if the rifle is loaded with a big conical bullet likely to punch right through a deer thirty or forty yards away, the animal should not travel far if your bullet hits where it is supposed to.

The same tactics used by conventional rifle hunters and archers also work for taking big game with a muzzleloader. Stand hunting—especially from trees—offers the best chance at placing an effective shot. Staying above the deer's natural line of sight allows the hunter some freedom to move just a little to keep comfortable during the often long wait without being spotted by the animals. Because they are less likely to be spooked,

Trapper Combo. A .50-caliber rifle and interchangeable 12-gauge smoothbore barrel. —Connecticut Valley Arms

Three recovered projectiles.
—*Thompson/Center*

deer taken from tree stands are usually browsing along slowly or moving at a natural gait. Hunters are more likely to place a good shot on a deer in these circumstances than on one moving at full throttle or on a jumped deer offering only its tail for a target.

The soft lead projectiles used in muzzleloading rifles are not brush busters, even though some of the big conical bullets might appear to be. The soft lead is easily deformed by anything it hits on the way to its target. A twig the diameter of common lead pencil is large enough to damage the bullet and send it into erratic flight. Making sure your shot is clear is as important as aligning your sight properly. Here again, if you shoot from an elevated stand—above most of the ground foliage, you'll have the advantage and are more likely to get a clear shot at a buck forty or fifty yards away.

Deer are creatures of habit. They follow the same trails and feed in the same areas day after day. Learning to read their signs will help you choose a good spot for your stand. In areas without much hunting pressure, deer probably won't deviate much from their daily routine, and any trail with considerable signs might eventually produce a good shot. However, in areas where deer are really pushed hard, especially on opening day or through the opening weekend of the season, smart old bucks make no bones about pulling up stakes and heading for less congested territory. This exodus from home range might be only temporary, but an old buck just does not like crowds.

When the pressure is on, an old, mossy-horned buck will look for secluded pockets of cover away from his normal haunts—an overgrown area or an isolated stand of pine trees—anywhere away from the army of hunters invading his home territory. Second guessing where an old buck will hole up can be pretty tricky. Your best bet is to look for tracks leading away from heavily hunted cover after the first day or two of the season.

Where seasons are split into two different periods, the smart hunter can set up an ambush for a

This Express rifle has .50-caliber side-by-side barrels. —*Connecticut Valley Arms*

buck on opening day of the second season. Chances are the buck will try the same tactics he used during the first half of the season. If he survives the entire season, he may try holing up in the same cover again the following year. Although an old buck might break from his daily routine, he is still a creature of habit.

Taking a deer or any big game animal with a rifle often referred to as "primitive" is a good feeling. It takes devotion to spend an entire season afield with a single-shot, front-loading rifle, knowing that your success for the entire season might rest on how well you place that one shot. This is part of the enjoyment of hunting with a muzzleloader—having the confidence to know that you will make that shot count when the time comes.

Packing a front-loading handgun as an accompaniment to, or as a back-up for, your muzzleloading long gun is an idea of long standing. Belt-carried hand cannon date back to the fourteenth century. Military use of handguns, particularly during the flint and percussion eras, proved that sidearms could serve effectively in battle—especially since single-shot muskets were the standard arms for soldiers of the time.

Black Powder Back-Up

Early hunters of dangerous game like the wild boar in Europe and the grizzly bears of the American frontier surely realized the advantages of having an emergency reserve shot handily tucked away in their waistbands or attached to their belts. Whenever possible, the mountain men of the Rockies latched onto a reliable sidearm. Most of the time they faced the dangers of the wilderness alone. More than one of these hardy individuals probably owed going to the big rendezvous in the sky with his scalp still intact to carrying a back-up for his heavy half-stock Plains rifle.

Using a muzzleloading sidearm to finish off wounded game is legal today in only a handful of states, so check your state game regulations carefully (see Appendix C). Even fewer allow black-powder pistols of any sort as the primary arm for big game hunting. As accurate as some of these guns might be, they just do not deliver the punch needed for downing even deer-sized game.

Hunters who commonly carry a black-powder pistol as an accompaniment to their rifle usually have both in the same caliber, allowing one size ball, one thickness of patch, and one granulation of black powder to serve both guns. A number of muzzleloader manufacturers and importers offer companion sidearms to some of their more popular front-loading rifle models. Lyman, Navy Arms, and Connecticut Valley Arms all produce single-shot muzzleloading handguns that match the caliber, ignition type, and general design of some of their best-selling rifles.

One problem that becomes immediately apparent to black-powder shooters when they first pack a muzzleloading handgun is how to carry the handgun safely and comfortably. Of course, you can stick the muzzle end of the barrel down into your waistband if your gun is not equipped with a belt hook, but packing a belt gun with an eight- or nine-inch barrel in this manner could become more than a little uncomfortable after several hours or several miles of walking. Some of the larger mail-order supply houses offer belt hooks for muzzleloading pistols. Generally these cost less than $15 and take ten or fifteen minutes to install; you might have to drill one or two holes. Another way to pack a pistol as a back-up is to fashion of holster of sorts, similar to those for the percussion revolvers.

An adjustable rear sight on a pistol carried in the field may not prove as desireable as a fixed sight. Many of the adjustable-type sights have a built-in coil spring, which maintains pressure against the bottom of the foundation bar. Tightening or loosening the adjustment screw raises and lowers the rear sight notch. But the constant jarring a pistol receives as it's carried can loosen the adjustment screw until it eventually falls out completely and becomes lost. A fixed rear sight makes good sense on a handgun that may be handled roughly. Once you sight the gun by filing either the top of the front sight blade or deepening the notch on the rear sight for elevation, and slightly tapping the rear sight one way or the other in its dovetailed slots for windage, the fixed sight is much less likely to lose alignment that the adjustable type, no matter how roughly you handle your weapon.

However you carry your pistol in the field, you probably should not carry it capped (if it's percussion) or primed (if it's flint), especially if you pack it inside your waistband. Always remember that when you carry a handgun right next to your body, the muzzle is usually pointed right at your thigh, leg, or foot. An accidental discharge could leave a nasty wound.

.54-caliber Plains pistol. —Lyman

Colt .45-caliber Buntline Special. This gun is in a class all by itself. Regardless of how it's carried, packing this one around all day would be uncomfortable. —Colt Firearms

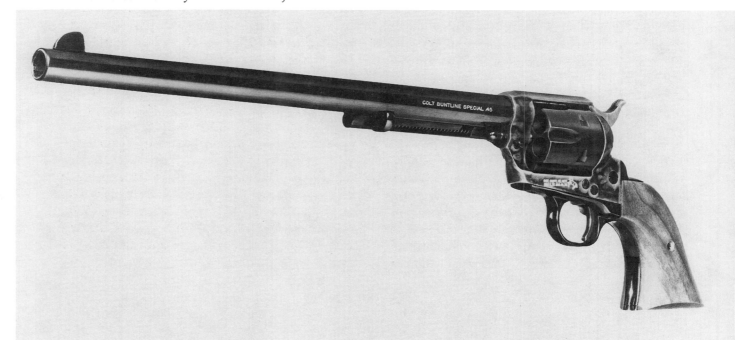

Remington .44-caliber New Army revolver. —*National Rifle Association.*

Loading Your Back-up Pistol

The short eight- or nine-inch barrel lengths common on guns of this type do not accommodate really heavy powder charges. The short barrel length means a hefty powder charge does not have enough time to burn completely before the bullet leaves the muzzle. In fact, the maximum efficient charge for a .50-caliber pistol with a nine-inch barrel is only about forty grains of FFFg black powder. The same barrel length in .54-caliber would probably burn between forty-five and fifty grains of FFFg. The light loads of black powder that burn completely inside the short barrel of a black-powder handgun do not produce the ballistics necessary to effectively drop any big game animal.

A forty-grain charge of FFFg will push a patched .490 round ball from the muzzle of a nine-inch .50-caliber barrel at approximately 950 fps and release about 450-500 foot-pounds of energy. While this is more than sufficient for placing a coup de grace on a down-but-not-out deer, antelope, elk, or even a sizeable black bear, it just isn't enough to war-

rant the use of the single-shot handgun as the main hunting arm for any of these game species.

Under controlled conditions a .44-caliber percussion revolver could be sufficient for hunting big game, mainly because these handguns offer quick, successive shots rather than a single shot like a muzzleloading handgun. The chambers of the big .44-caliber percussion Walker revolver reproductions can be stuffed with up to fifty grains of FFFg, which will push a tight-fitting .454-diameter 141-grain round ball from the muzzle of a nine-inch barrel at almost 1,200 fps, with 450 foot-pounds of muzzle energy. This is still a far cry from being a potent big game load, but shooting game species like wild boar or even black bear hunted with hounds generally takes place from very close range. A black-powder handgunner familiar with the handling characteristics of his or her percussion revolver could quickly place several good hits into the target. Then, even if the game broke and ran after being solidly hit, the hounds could stick with the animal until the hunter can make a finishing shot.

CHAPTER 8

SMALL GAME

Rifles

Recent years have witnessed a resurgence in hunting small game and varmints with muzzleloaders. Hunting deer and other big game with front-loading rifles has inspired hunters to test their skills against rabbits, squirrels, raccoons, woodchucks, badgers, and other smaller prey. Shooting black powder is definitely contagious; once hunters discover just how much fun hunting with an old-fashioned front-loader really is, many turn to muzzleloading for at least some of their other hunting.

Fortunately, muzzleloading manufacturers and importers have realized this important segment of the market. Since the 1980s they have introduced a number of well-made, accurate small-bore front-loading rifles designed primarily for hunting small game. Properly loaded, most of these rifles can produce amazing one-hole groups at distances appropriate for taking small game.

The criteria for a small game muzzleloading rifle are simple: it should have a small bore and propel a light sphere of lead with a light powder charge. The whole idea is to turn the prey into table fare, not to pulverized it into shred of inedible meat (unless, of course, you're shooting varmints, in which case it doesn't much matter). Until the recent surge of interest in shooting small-bore rifles, most hunters tried to "load down" their front-loading deer rifles for use on small

game. Even with light charges (20-25 grains) of FFFg, the .45- and .50-caliber rifles are just too destructive on small game to be practical. Even a .40 caliber slug will destroy considerably the edible portions of squirrels and rabbits.

From time to time custom muzzleloading rifle manufacturers have offered barrels bored as small as .25 caliber, but such tiny bores can be problematic to load. Exceptionally small bores foul easily and can be very touchy about even the slightest variation in powder charges. Small game hunters might better concentrate on one of the readily available .32- or .36-caliber reproduction rifles. Some of these include the Thompson/Center Seneca in .32 caliber, the Dixie Gun Works .32-caliber Tennessee Squirrel rifle, and the Navy Arms .32- and .36-caliber Mule Ear side-hammer rifle. All of these modern reproductions are exceptionally well made and, when loaded properly, can deliver head-shot accuracy for most small game at reasonable distances.

For the greatest accuracy, a small-bore black-powder rifle should feature a relatively fast rifling twist. Until just a few years ago, most barrel makers paid little attention to .32- and .36-caliber barrels. No one seemed to take seriously the small-caliber rifles intended almost exclusively for use on small game. As a result, practically all custom barrels came with slow rifling twists of about one

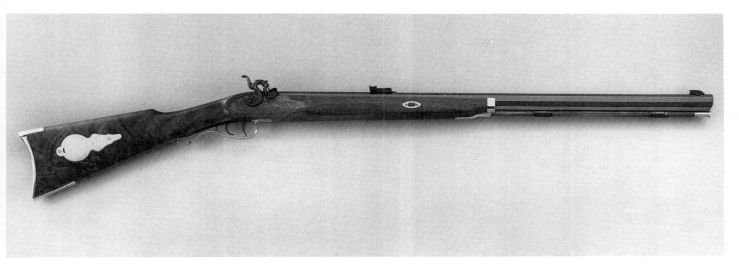

.32-caliber Seneca percussion rifle. Small bores can foul quickly. —Thompson/Center

turn in sixty-six inches. These perform accurately with a patched round ball, but they require a fairly hefty powder charge. Such a rifled barrel in .32 caliber may require up to forty grains of FFFg for peak performance. That much powder in a barrel forty-one and a half inches long, like that found on Dixie's small-bore muzzleloading rifle, discharges with a muzzle velocity of just over 2,000 feet per second (fps) and muzzle energy of about 425 foot-pounds. Ballistically, the light forty-four-grain .310-diameter ball fired in a .32-caliber rifle is pushed from the long barrel at velocities and energies comparable to a .22-caliber magnum rimfire. A center hit on a bushytail or cottontail could ruin it as potential table fare. That's a waste of good game.

Powder charges of twenty to twenty-five grains of FFFg are more appropriate for .32- and .36-caliber rifles. Although still a little slow for optimum accuracy from small-bore barrels, most modern reproductions feature a faster rifling twist rate of one turn in forty-eight to fifty-six inches. In larger guns of .45 or .50 caliber, this would be quite a fast rate of twist; but in .32- or .36-caliber rifles it is not. One rifle recently designed along these lines is the Thompson/Center Cherokee. With an even faster rate of twist (one turn in thirty inches), this .32-caliber front-loader produces game-getting accuracy at twenty-five yards with powder charges as light as fifteen grains. The Cherokee's twenty-four-inch barrel charged with twenty grains of FFFg produces a muzzle velocity

.32-caliber Cherokee. This half-stock is patterened after early New England hunting rifles. —Thompson/Center

of about 1,475 fps and just over 200 foot-pounds of muzzle energy. This is roughly equivalent to the ballistics of some .22-caliber long-rifle ammunition and is ideal for most small game hunting.

Practically all custom barrel makers offer both cut-rifled and button-rifled bores with twist rates of about one turn in forty-eight inches for .32 and .36 calibers. In the .32-caliber barrels with this rate of twist, powder charges of twenty-five grains often turn in the best performance, but such a load may prove a little too destructive on edible game. A .36-caliber rifle loaded with about thirty grains of FFFg is actually better suited for critters slightly larger than squirrels and rabbits. Generally, when hunting small game you'll want to use the lightest effective charge.

Ignitions systems pose another consideration in hunting small game. When shooting at a quick-moving target, such as a squirrel's head, a fast, positive ignition increases your odds of hitting the target. Except for those purists who use flintlocks for everything, most muzzleloading hunters rely on the percussion system for small game. In fact, a very small percentage of the reproduction rifles in .32 and .36 caliber offer any choice; most are available in percussion only.

Some hunters rely on a drum-and-nipple arrangement or a bolster-type breech; these designs position the nipple off to one side of the barrel. When the hammer strikes the percussion cap, the fire must make a sharp turn before it enters the breech end of the bore for ignition. Other designs, such as the under-hammer and side-slapper or mule-ear locks are also available. With these systems, the nipple threads directly into the side of the barrel. Fire from the cap enters the breech to the powder charge in a straight line, and ignition is spontaneous. The under-hammer design swings the hammer forward from underneath the gun to strike the nipple on the bottomside of the barrel, usually immediately in front of the trigger guard. The mule-ear hammer swings horizontally, hitting the nipple threaded into the side of the barrel.

Most small bores generally perform very well with a ball .010 inch less than the bore size; for instance, use a .310-diameter ball in a .32 caliber, and a .350-diameter ball in a .36 caliber. With such undersized balls, patching material in thicknesses of .010-.015 inch works best. Dixie Gun Works recommends using a .310 or .315 ball in its .32-caliber long rifle. With the smaller .310-diameter ball, use .010-.015 patching to take up the void;

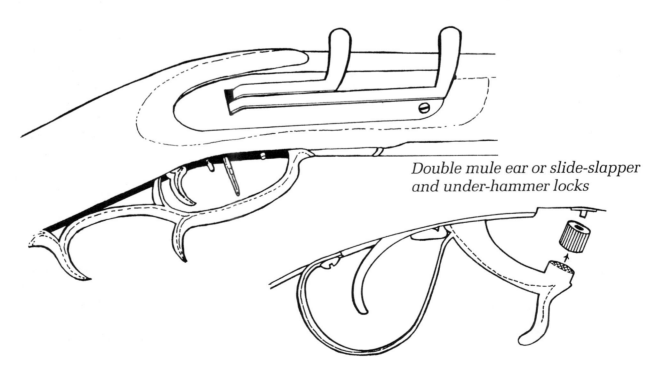

Double mule ear or slide-slapper and under-hammer locks

with the larger .315-diameter ball, patching any thicker than .005 might make loading extremely difficult.

Small-bore rifles are notorious for fouling easily, since the shallow grooves quickly fill with powder residue. To keep a .32- or .36-caliber rifle performing at its peak throughout your hunt, wipe the bore clean after each and every shot. Many reproduction guns come with a ramrod fitted to accept a cleaning jag at its threaded tip. It only takes a couple of seconds to run a saliva-dampened patch down the bore and back out. The patch should be damp, not wet. If you accidentally run an over-saturated patch through, wipe out the excess moisture by following it with a dry patch. The idea is to wipe away just enough of the fouling to make loading easy, not to clean the bore spotless. Many hunters leave the cleaning jag threaded into the ramrod tip all the time. It adds an inch or so to the length of the ramrod, making it easier to grasp and pull from the thimbles without being so long as to become a nuisance in the field.

The ramrods of small-bore front-loaders have to be thin to fit inside the pip-squeak bores. Traditionally, a 5/16-inch-diameter rod is appropriate for most .32- or .36-caliber bores. A hardwood rod this thin, even if it's turned from straight-grained hickory, can become fatigued and snap under the stress of a really tight patch and ball. Mountain State Muzzleloading Supplies of Williamstown, West Virginia, has remedied this problem with its Super-Rod, made of wood-colored plastic. These rods are flexible enough to resist breakage, yet stiff enough to exert sufficient pressure on the patched ball for loading. Mountain State offers replacement Super-Rods for Dixie's .32-caliber Tennessee Squirrel rifle and Thompson/Center's .36-caliber Seneca and .32-caliber Cherokee. Although only one tip is actually necessary, Super-Rods come with a tip on each end, one threaded for 8x32 jags and accessories, the other threaded for 10x32 accessories. If your barrel is shorter than the Dixie .32-caliber Squirrel rifle, you can still use a Super-Rod by cutting it to length, leaving the preferred tip intact.

Some hunters avoid the fouling problem by shooting Pyrodex instead of black powder. Unlike black powder, Pyrodex fouling does not continue to build with each shot. The first shot with this black-powder substitute leaves some fouling in the bore, but not enough to hamper loading. Successive shots do not add to the amount of fouling in the barrel.

The main drawback to Pyrodex is that it is a little harder to ignite than FFFg black powder. Even the fine-grained P grade, which works best in small bores, requires a hot flash for reliable ignition. When shooting Pyrodex in a percussion rifle, install a vented Uncle Mike's Hot-Shot nipple. The design of the Hot-Shot allows nearly twice the flash produced by standard unvented nipples to enter the bore. When you use Pyrodex in a flintlock rifle, first drop a few grains of FFFg or FFFFg in through the muzzle—enough to ensure that some reaches the point where the vent hole enters the bore—and then pour in the Pyrodex charge. Surprisingly, the burning Pyrodex seems to consume the fouling normally left by even a small amount of black powder. Prime the pan of a flintlock the same as if you were using black powder alone.

Perhaps the greatest compromise of accuracy in a small-bore rifle is inconsistent powder charges. Behind a light .44-grain, .310 round ball or even a 65-grain, .350 round ball, a half-grain variation in powder volume could result in the ball hitting an inch high or low at twenty-five yards—enough to miss a target as small as a bushytail's head.

When filling your measure with powder, always tap it lightly to settle the grains and try to level it the same each and every time. This ensures that you load a consistent measure of powder into the barrel for each shot. The lighter the charge, the more important it is to get it exact every time. Powder itself is not always the same from one can to another. Before taking a new can of powder on a hunt, test it by putting a few rounds through your rifle to make sure it still prints bullets in the same place.

One advantage of shooting the small bores is the economics involved. If you shoot twenty-grain charges of FFFg in a .32-caliber rifle, you should get 350 shots from a pound of powder. Load Pyrodex in volumes equivalent to your black powder charges. Since it is bulkier by volume, a pound can of Pyrodex should yeild an even higher number of shots than black powder.

Muzzleloading hunters often find they can steal upon a tree with several squirrels feeding in its lofty branches. It is possible to drop several squirrels from the same tree. The secret is to reload as quickly as possible without causing too much commotion. One way to do this is to use a loading block. This is simply a piece of wood with a row of holes drilled about the same diameter as your bore size. Place patched balls into the holes ahead of time. When you want to reload, simply align one of these loads over your muzzle, then push the patched ball into your bore with your short starter. The block eliminates fumbling around for balls and patches. You can also premeasure powder charges in capped plastic tubes to trim your reloading time considerably.

Hunting with a rifle of any sort might not appeal to some hunters. In many parts of the country, using a rifle on small game may be illegal. But this doesn't mean muzzleloading enthusiasts have to miss out on the thrill of hunting small game. With the right loads, a muzzleloading scattergun can take game at least as effectively as a muzzleloading rifle. In most cases, a muzzleloading smoothbore may actually increase your chances of taking the game you're after. Navy Arms, Dixie Gun Works, and several other firms offer a wide variety of muzzleloading shotguns for hunting. For more information on hunting with scatterguns, see the following chapter.

1861 Colt .36-caliber Navy revolver. Good for turning small game into tablefare. —National Rifle Association

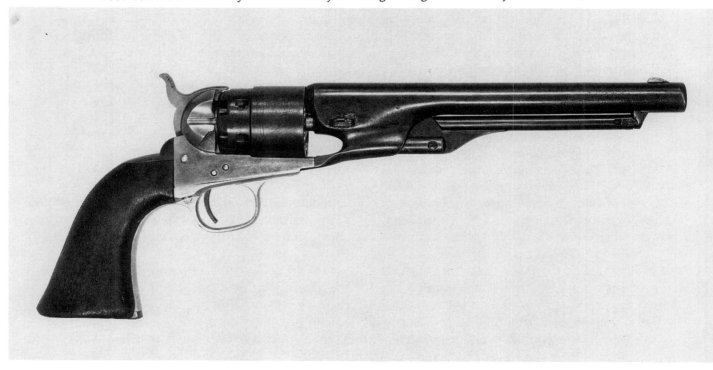

Handguns

Although they are not suitable for hunting big game, black-powder handguns are plenty adequate for downing even large predators like coyotes and varmints like woodchucks, and, in the hands of an expert, excellent for taking small game. In fact, hunting any of these species with a front-loading handgun can provide black-powder hunters with all the challenge they can handle.

Adjustable-type sights are a viable advantage for black-powder handguns, which are less apt to get knocked around too much if you carry the gun as the primary arm while hunting small game. On a handgun, these sights allow you to make the precise adjustments necessary for often downsized targets.

A solid hit with a .451 or .457 round ball shot through a .44-caliber percussion revolver could prove devastating to the edible portions of a cottontail or bushytail. Head shot accuracy is a must! To turn small game into table fare, a .31- or .36-caliber percussion revolver is ideal. Not only are the lighter spheres much easier on game, but these handguns, when carried as secondary arms for occasional close-up sitting shots, are a lot easier to pack around all day. The little .31-caliber Colt pocket model reproductions often weigh less than one-and-a-half pounds while the .36-caliber Colt 1851 Navy models weigh only about a pound more.

Hunting with handguns of all types has increased in popularity in recent years. And black-powder handguns are no exception. Many shooters go to great lengths just to prove the accuracy of their black-powder pistols. As a result, it is not uncommon nowadays to see handgun scopes solidly affixed to the top straps of percussion revolvers or the top flats of a single-shot muzzleloading handgun barrels. Although not really a traditional-looking rig, a scoped black powder handgun can amaze even the purist black-powder burner with its accuracy.

Black-powder handguns are second only to muzzleloading rifles in popularity. Millions have been produced since the late 1950s, yet few are ever seen in the field. And, that's a real shame since hunting with one of these handguns can offer muzzleloading hunters another dimension in black-powder sport.

Since small game seasons usually last several months, small game hunters get more time afield than those pursuing big game. Modern hunters are more likely out for the challenge of the sport than for meat. With decreasing limits and shorter seasons, hunting with muzzleloaders makes more sense now than ever before; it allows you to extract the utmost enjoyment from a limited resource. And besides, it's very satisfying to take your limit of rabbits or bushytails with a gun that's been out-of-date for more than a century.

CHAPTER 9

SHOTGUNS

Chokes and Patterns

The shotgun owes the longevity of its popularity primarily to the fact that it was developed as a hunter's tool and requires no great skill to master. Unlike a rifle or handgun, the "scattergun" is not a precision instrument for long-range accuracy. It was designed for taking game at close range with a fast, sometimes haphazardly aimed shot. The gauge of a shotgun is measured by the number of round lead balls (equal in diameter to its bore) required to weigh one pound; thus, the smaller-numbered gauge indicates a larger-diameter bore. For the more common muzzleloading gauges, this measurement translates to inches as follows:

Gauge	Bore Diameter (inch)
10	.775
11	.751
12	.729
13	.710
16	.662
20	.615
28	.550

During the heyday of muzzleloading shotguns, approximately 1820 to about 1860, the effects of a choked bore were not really understood. Some makers realized that if they constricted the muzzle slightly, the shot held together in a tighter pattern at longer ranges. A few remaining originals from this period display very radical attempts to make a smoothbore weapon more effective at long ranges. Dixie Gun Works, one of the largest antique arms dealers in the country, once had on display (and for sale) an original twin-bore, percussion Manton double that featured bores measuring a true 10 gauge at the muzzle, but closer to 8 gauge (.835) at the breech end. Its long 36-38-inch twin bores tapered their full length!

The trouble with loading such an eccentrically choked barrel is the fact that the gun is still a muzzleloader. Wads that fit tightly through the muzzle fit too loosely to be really effective by the time they reach the powder charge near the breach, where the bore is larger than at the muzzle. The Manton double must have been designed to accept loose wadding, or tow, as it was called in those days. After shooters measured a powder charge and poured it in, they shredded loose wadding through the bore and retamped it into a cushioned wad over the powder charge. They then poured in the shot and tamped a thin layer of tow over it to keep the pellets from running back out in case the muzzle got pointed downward.

To load a gun in such a manner must have been very time-consuming. Since this particular percussion double weighed about fourteen pounds and was built with a massive breech for shooting exceptionally heavy powder charges, it was prob-

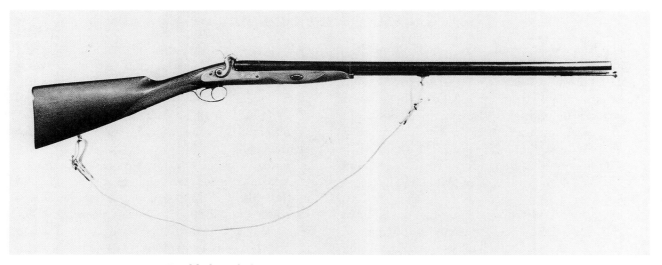

Double-barreled 12-gauge percussion shotgun. —Dixie Gun Works

ably designed for hunting large waterfowl, such as geese or swans. Shooting from a blind, the hunter could lay everything out for convenience and quicker loading.

A constriction, or choke, of any sort in the muzzle of a front-loading scattergun can hamper its loading. For that reason, the vast majority of the fine original shotguns that once flowed from shops in England, several areas in Europe, and even the United States, were built with "cylinder-bore" barrels—equal in diameter at both the muzzle and the breach. A few of these guns featured what is commonly referred to as a "jug choke," in which the bore is choked several inches from the muzzle. The cylinder-bore muzzle acted as a funnel of sorts, allowing the shooter to stuff in wads quickly and easily during loading. A healthy push with the ramrod would force wads down the barrel and through the jug choke.

A true cylinder-bore muzzleloading shotgun loads very easily. Surprisingly, shot patterns can be opened or tightened considerably simply by regulating how the gun is loaded. One combination of powder charge, wads, and shot will result in open patterns for close-cover work while another combination will achieve tighter patterns for longer-range shots.

Sustained pressure at the rear of the shot column (from the over-powder and/or cushioned wads) as the pellets leave the muzzle is key to achieving a wide-open shot spread. A heavy shot load resists being pushed; and when the shot leaves the muzzle, the wad tends to push through the load of pellets. Without the barrel walls to hold the shot together, it reacts to the sustained pressure of the wad behind it by moving outward slightly instead of maintaining its straight-ahead flight. Denser wads maintain greater velocity, producing wider open patterns.

Most cylinder-bore barrels loaded with approximately 20 percent more shot by volume than powder will result in patterns printing only 30 to 35 percent of the load inside a thirty-inch circle at thirty yards. If you use too much powder, the wad may push all the way through the shot load before losing its velocity and dropping to the ground. If this happens, holes (blank areas) might appear in the center of your pattern.

For tighter patterns from a cylinder-bore muzzleloading shotgun, load nearly equal volumes of powder and shot. Many old-timers relied on the same measure for dumping both powder and shot into the muzzle of their front-loading smoothbores. Loaded with the right combination of wads, some cylinder-bore shotgun barrels can reliably produce patterns that print upwards of 60 to 65 percent of the shot load inside a thirty-inch circle at thirty yards.

Loading Your Shotgun

Loading a scattergun takes a little more time than loading a rifle. It's not more complicated; it's just that more stuff has to go through the muzzle: the measured powder goes first, then a heavy card wad (.125-inch thick) followed by a half-inch thick cushioned wad, then the shot charge, and finally the over-shot card wad (.030-inch thick). To complete the loading process you must cap the nipple on a percussion gun or prime the flash pan if you have a flintlock.

Locating a ready source of shotgun wads is not always easy. Wads for reloading the old paper-style shells do not work well for muzzleloaders. Designed to be loaded into a hull or shell casing, these wads normally fit too loosely in a muzzleloading barrel of the same gauge. It is, however, fairly easy to cut suitable wads for your muzzleloader from materials readily available. You can punch the thick over-powder card wads from old cigar boxes; cut the cushion wads from scrap pieces of black insulation board or ceiling tile; and fashion the thin over-shot cards from boxes for shoes or cereal. Most of the larger mail-order black-powder supply firms offer complete lines of wad punches that will easily render wads from any of these materials. To cut the card wads, stack several layers on top of one another and punch out five or six wads in a single blow. Commercially produced shotgun wads are also available.

Wads, especially the half-inch thick cushion wads when dipped into a mixture of beeswax and mutton tallow, help to seal off the powder charge from any moisture that may enter the muzzle. The wax-tallow mixture liquefies to some extent when fired and helps to keep fouling soft in the barrel for easier loading of subsequent shots. Another way to waterproof a load and keep fouling soft is to squirt a small amount of grease-like commercial lube between the heavy over-powder card wad and the cushion wad. Although muzzleloading shotguns are not as notorious as some rifles for fouling to the point where loading becomes almost impossible, a little lube does make loading less tedious. Just don't use too much.

The author firing a Hawken-type long rifle.
—*D. Juris-Stetser*

Scatterguns for Hunting

Quality reproduction muzzleloading shotguns did not appear on the market until the early 1970s, when Navy Arms, Richland Arms, and Dixie Gun Works all introduced well-built, lightweight, side-by-side 12 gauges; the basic style is still available from several firms today. These exceptionally well-made percussion shotguns have one serious strike against them—the light weight. At a mere six and a half pounds, the side-by-side is a real dream to carry afield for a daylong hunt, but its more than a little painful to shoot when loaded with hefty hunting charges. Thousands have been sold, and, with the proper loads, they are fine upland bird guns.

Some shooters have remedied the gun's recoil problem to some extent by adding a pound of weight to the stock. To do this, remove the butt plate and drill a few holes into the butt, then insert short bars of lead into the holes; wrapping them in cloth first keeps them from rattling around after you've reinstalled the butt plate. Many a black-powder shotgunner has also installed a recoil reducer or two—like those employed by modern trap shooters—to remedy the painful recoil of an otherwise fine-handling shotgun.

Most of the lightweight doubles feature 28-inch barrels in choked and cylinder-bore styles. Generally, when loaded in equal volumes with about seventy grains of FFg and 1.125 ounces of shot, obeying the proper sequence of wads, these doubles print about 50 percent of their shot loads inside a thirty-inch circle at thirty yards. Such performance is ideal for hunting most upland game birds or cottontails, where shots from twenty to thirty yards are common. With powder charges of eighty grains or more of FFg, these doubles become more painful to handle.

Some importers offer heftier doubles designed primarily for hunters, especially those who need heavy charges suitable for waterfowl and turkeys. Most of the heavyweight 12-gauge side-by-sides have cylinder-bore barrels about thirty inches long. These guns generally weigh about eight pounds and can handle being stoked up with considerably larger loads.

The magnum model 12-gauge doubles available from Navy Arms, Dixie Gun Works, and a few other makers perform very well with heavy hunting charges of between ninety and a hundred grains of FFg behind as much as one and a half ounces of shot. Loaded as earlier described, these smoothbore doubles print about 50 percent of their shot loads at thirty yards. The open patterns common to most muzzleloading shotgun reproductions can prove beneficial for hunting rabbits or upland birds in thick cover. But shooting a big

A 12-gauge Caplock shotgun. Rabbits and squirrels simmered together in the same pot make "game pie." In the olden days, muzzleloading shotguns were responsible for most of those pies. —Thompson/Center

*Stalking wild turkeys with a
12-gauge muzzleloader.*
—*Wyoming Game and Fish Dept.*

old Canadian honker or wild turkey gobbler from 35-40 yards with only 50 percent of your pellets hitting the mark just won't do the job.

One way to tighten your patterns considerably is to load with a homemade shot cup using the hull of a plastic shotgun shell. This prevents your pellets from spreading out so soon after they leave the muzzle. To form the cup, first crimp the empty hull, then cut off the brass base and head. Cut the plastic hull even with the brass base on high-brass hulls to keep the cup as long as possible. Next, cut three short fold-out wings a half-inch long and a quarter-inch wide into the sides of the plastic hull. Leave these attached to the hull along the edge of the crimp that now forms the bottom of the shot cup.

Load the shot cup into your shotgun muzzle directly on top of the cushioned wad that retains your powder charge. The wings should remain in place along the sides of the hull as you insert the plastic cup into the muzzle. Dump your shot charge into the cup before pushing it down the bore with the ramrod to visually ensure none of the pellets get behind the folding wings. The shot-filled cup should seat easily over the cushioned wad. Top off the load a thin (.030 thick) card wad to keep the shot from rolling back out the muzzle if you point the gun downward.

When you fire, the wing slits will open up as soon as the cup leaves the muzzle. The plastic cup falls away about fifteen feet past the muzzle, allowing your shot charge to hold together well about twenty yards beyond the muzzle, after which it begins to open up. This keeps your pattern tighter for longer shots. If you don't cut wing slits, the shot charge won't spread out and might punch a hole, like a slug would, in your target as far as thirty yards away.

Use a 28-gauge hull to make a shot cup for a 20-gauge front-loader; a 20-gauge hull for a 16-gauge front-loading smoothbore, such as the .69-caliber flintlock Charleville musket reproductions; and a 16-gauge hull for a .751-caliber smoothbore, such as the Brown Bess flint musket reproductions and some of the true 11-gauge doubles currently being sold as percussion 10-gauge shotguns.

Occasionally, the plastic one-piece wad units for reloading modern 12-gauge shot shells will work well in reproduction 12-gauge doubles. It's always worth a try to see if a particular gun will pattern well with them since they do make loading a lot easier. Always avoid using plastic wads with a flimsy base or a wad column that collapses easily. Remington's Power Piston wads seem to work the best in a muzzleloading shotgun. For good results, it's often best to use only the shot cup portion of these units, trimming off and discarding the bases. Shot cups slit only about a third of the way down produce the tightest patterns. When using the cup portion of plastic wad units, load the cups over the cushion wad in the same manner as the shot cup formed from a shot-shell hull. If you use the entire one-piece plastic wad, don't place the heavy card or cushion wads over the powder charge.

Several firms offer big percussion doubles usually labeled as a 10 gauge, but the bore measurements reveal them actually as 11 gauges. In gauge size, these doubles do not normally offer shooters any advantage over the heavyweight 12-gauge models; but the added heft of the barrels and overall weight of the 11-gauge bore "10-gauge" doubles does allow hunters with low pain thresholds to shoot charges heavy enough to make the difference between dropping a Canadian honker at thirty-five yards or simply watching it fly away.

Some of these big-bore shotgun models come with double beads, one at the muzzle and a another about halfway down the wide ridge bridging the twin cylinder-bore tubes. The sighting arrangement is ideal for precisely placing a load of No. 2 or No. 4 shot at a wild turkey-gobbler's head. Serious turkey hunters should consider using one of these thirty-inch barrel doubles, which perform nicely with a much as 110 grains of FFg behind shot loads as hefty as one and three-quarter ounces.

If you fire only one barrel and want to reload, you will be wise to uncap the unfired barrel before reloading the empty one. It is extremely dangerous to stand over the muzzle of a loaded barrel while reloading. Most black-powder hunters carry the double afield with the hammers at half-cock. But this does not ensure that the gun is completely safe and free from accidental discharge. No mechanical device is that perfect. However, carrying a double with the hammers at half-cock reduces the chance of an accidental discharge if the gun is dropped or if you stumble. The half-cock position can also prevent the unfired barrel from self-discharging, which it might as the gun recoils from a heavy hunting charge if the hammer on the unfired side is carried completely down on top of the percussion cap.

A young hunter connects with his muzzleloading shotgun.
—*Wyoming Game and Fish Dept.*

Rifle-Shotgun Conversion Barrels

The popularity of an interchangeable barrel system utilizing a hooked breech for several of today's more popular half-stock rifles has spurred some manufacturers to produce drop-in shotgun barrels. Most of these so-called drop-in replacement barrels were designed to fit the Thompson/Center Hawken rifle, but they also work on a number of other brand-name half-stocks of similar styling, especially those produced in Italy.

Limited by the barrel diameters of most contemporary Hawken rifles, these drop-in shotgun barrels are available in twenty-four and twenty-eight gauge. Although small in bore size, the 32-34-inch drop-ins produce some pretty impressive patterns. When you load with a heavy card wad placed directly over the powder followed by a cushioned wad, the shot charge, and a thin over-shot card wad, the resulting pattern will generally print better than 50 to 60 percent of the shot load inside a thirty-inch circle at thirty yards. This is slightly less impressive when one takes into account that most shot loads in a smoothbore of this size usually weigh less than an ounce and proper

charges of about fifty grains of FFg are common. Still, you can count on the Hawken replacement barrel for close-range, stationary cottontails and squirrels, and it adds to the versatility of your muzzleloader.

Many antique scatterguns are small gauge. In fact, early-day flint shotguns with bores larger than 15 gauge were uncommon; most were closer to 20 gauge. But, other than the drop-in barrels offered for the Hawken rifles, few small-bore shotgun reproductions are currently available. Barrel length is extremely important to pattern density with smoothbores of 20 gauge or smaller The longer the barrel, generally, the tighter the pattern. The longer shot string provided by the longer barrel could become a handicap in wing shooting; but with a longer barrel the pellets are all headed in the same direction and, on stationary targets like squirrels or turkeys, could produce a better game-killing pattern than pellets shot from one of the shorter-barreled, larger-gauge smoothbores.

Hawken .54-caliber caplock. This is one of the most copied rifles in the history of firearms. —Thompson/Center

Other Reproductions

Anyone looking for a flintlock smoothbore will not find much of a selection. However, several copies of the Brown Bess musket, at least one reproduction of the Charleville smoothbore musket, and a copy of the Indian trade gun are available—and all of them can handle a shot charge very effectively.

Most of the Brown Bess copies are .75 caliber, with bores measuring right at .751 inch, making the long forty-two-inch barrel a true 11 gauge. When loaded with a series of card and felt wads as described earlier, these big flintlocks make excellent fowlers. Although the barrel wall at the muzzle appears exceptionally thin, the Brown Bess copies are built with a very heavy-walled barrel at the breech. Powder charges of 80-90 grains and shot charges of one and a quarter to one and a half ounces discharge safely through the long barrels. Remember, the long length of the flint smoothbore's barrel generally result in a strung-out shot string. Although patterns fired on paper may appear nice and tight, the long shot string does not put a lot of pellets up at the leading edge of the pattern, making it just a little iffy for shooting at fast-moving targets.

True to the originals, the modern copies of the Charleville flint musket, available from several firms in the past and still available from Navy Arms, come with an exceptionally long (slightly over forty-four and a half inches) .69-caliber smoothbore barrel. The .690-inch bore of this flintlock makes the Charleville a suitable 14 gauge. The measurement for a true 14 gauge is .693 inch, but the bore of the Charleville is so close that wads for the 14 gauge work nicely. The extra-long barrel also means a longer shot string, but patterns thrown with the big military flinter are generally very good. A 70-80-grain charge of FFg behind 1.125 ounces of shot produces a very acceptable hunting pattern.

One of the very first all-purpose guns was the flint smoothbore that came to be known as the Indian trade gun. As the name implies, these guns were designed for trade with the North American Indians by such fur-trading outfits as the Northwest Company and the Hudson's Bay Company. Smoothbores loaded with shot make hitting a target much easier than those loaded with a single patched round ball. Indians who never fired a firearm before in their lives could learn the fundamentals of shooting (with a load of bird shot) in a matter of a few rounds.

The white trappers, especially those who became known as mountain men, appreciated the versatility of guns they could load with either shot or a patched round ball. They could take both large and small game with a single firearm, and in tight situations in hostile country they

.54-caliber New Englander-style flintlock rifle. —Thompson/Center

could fire and reload these weapons much more quickly than they could a rifle that required a patched ball.

Most original Indian trade muskets came with 20 gauge or smaller barrels; 24 gauge was popular in both English and French models. Although a few existing originals sported barrels about 30 inches, longer barrels of 36-44 inches were more common. Loaded in the same manner as the Brown Bess or Charleville smoothbore muskets, most longer-barreled Indian trade guns produce tighter patterns at thirty yards. Shooting guns of this type is now the focus of renewed interest; and more and more black-powder shooters, especially buckskinners, are relying on the long-barreled smoothbores for at least some of their shooting and hunting.

Many trade gunners install a set of low-profiled Kentucky-type sights on the barrels and sight in the muskets with a patched round ball. Patterns produced by a load of shot are somewhat forgiving; the same gun that prints a patched ball nearly dead-on at fifty yards might only center a shot pattern a few inches above the point of aim at twenty-five or thirty yards. Although both the Brown Bess and Charleville muskets can also throw a patched round ball fairly accurately, they lack suitable sighting systems. Neither musket comes with a back sight of any sort, and the front sight of the Brown Bess is a huge square lug that doubles for attaching a bayonet.

Because there are no rifling grooves into which a patch can compress, any smoothbore will take a round ball considerably smaller in diameter than at first seems reasonable. A 20-gauge bore (.615 diameter) accepts and shoots well a .600 round ball; a 12-gauge (.729 diameter) requires a .715 ball for best performance; a 10-gauge (.775 inch) does best with a .730 or .735 ball. A percussion double loaded with shot in one barrel and a patched ball in the other is ready for just about anything.

Whichever gun you choose, you cannot beat the enjoyment of shooting a muzzleloading scattergun.

EPILOGUE

Living History

Black-powder shooting sports have given rise to several areas of specialized interest, most notably rendezvous, skirmishes, and camp reenactments, all of which allow the participants to relive history. Easily the most popular of the three, rendezvous by the hundred are held across the country each year; some attract several thousand participants and even more curious onlookers thirsting to know more about the past.

Rendezvous originally grew out of the need for a central meeting point and trading forum. North American frontiersmen established gatherings in the Rocky Mountains to trade, visit, and test their skills in friendly matches with one another during the height of the fur trade. Trappers in the 1820s and 1830s made good money compared to working stiffs back in the states. But mountain prices for trade goods—ammunition and blankets, traps and horses, tobacco and liquor, and the foofaraw to remind the men of female culture—were outrageous. Most mountain men spent more money (or its equivalent in furs) in a few weeks at the rendezvous than their city cousins made in as many years.

The rendezvous was a political, economic, and social microcosm that helped shape the American character and nation—a tiny, temporary oasis of civilization in a vast wilderness. But the main business of rendezvous was the exchange of furs for supplies so the mountain men would not have to trek across the Great Plains to the usual marketplace—St. Louis. When felt hats made from beaver pelts went out of style and the demand for furs dwindled, the annual rendezvous died out. But the spirit of the meetings did not.

Modern rendezvous-goers party as hard as their forbearers did over 150 years ago; and, if that's what you want, you'll get plenty at these meetings scattered across the country. But they are also family outings for many, and the revelers respect that. These events celebrate one of the most colorful periods of American history—a time remembered as the Fur Trade era. It witnessed the opening of the American West and has proven ideal for the incurable romantic who wants not only to study the period, but to live the part for a couple of days, a week, or even a month each year. The annual gatherings commemorate the era of the mountain men, arguably one of our nation's most adventurous and exciting times.

The largest modern rendezvous encampments takes place in conjunction with the spring and fall shoots at the National Muzzleloading Rifle Association range in Friendship, Indiana. These shoots normally attract from 12,000 to 20,000 campers, approximately half of whom choose to camp in "primitive" style. The division between the modern campers and the rendezvous encampment is

Primitive rendezvous camp in South Dakota. —*South Dakota Tourism*

Period dress is required in some encampments. —*Les Mann, Chadron (Nebraska) Record*

clear. While a few early-type shelters may dot row upon row of modern travel trailers and tents, only camps authentic to styles of the early nineteenth century or before can be set up in the primitive camping area.

Not only are the camps genuine in design, the inhabitants must wear clothing appropriate to the period. Proper styles of dress include early colonial attire, Revolutionary War uniforms, and buckskins. The latter is a favorite, since these outfits are generally handmade and allow the maker-wearers to express a great deal of individuality in the assembly of their outfits. The hides that make up their clothing often are taken from game they personally harvested. Walking through a primitive camp can be like walking back in history 150 years or more.

The primitive camp at the national range is just one of the several such gatherings sanctioned by the National Muzzleloading Rifle Association. The organization also helps to sponsor regional rendezvous in the West, Midwest, East, and Southeast each year. Some of these camps are open only to those who wear period costumes; others allow, or at least have one day set aside for, outside visitors. The reason is not that buckskinners are such recluses, but that they seriously want to maintain the authentic flavor of their get-togethers by having everyone participate, right down to the clothes on his or her back.

A typical day in these primitive camps starts as the sun climbs. The "booshway" (a wilderness variant of the capitalistic "bourgeois"), or his representative, solicits donations from the traders and craftsmen for prizes in the competitions. You could say it's part of the overhead, like taxes. But the items are given gladly—truly in the spirit of a donation. The competitive events are informal

Sharing the craft with youngsters at Fort Sisseton, South Dakota.
—Mary DeWitt

Settling in for an evening beside the fire at the Chadron, Nebraska, Rendezvous. —Les Mann, Chadron Record

and usually divided into separate categories for men, women, and children.

Shooting matches are normally elimination events. By turns, shooters step up to a stick on the ground that marks the firing line, then pot away offhandedly at, say, a skillet hanging in a tree or some other target. Miss and you're out. The firing line moves farther away for the survivors, and they do it again and again until only one remains to take the prize.

Other events include such contests as the stake shoot, a team event that tests firepower—the first team to shoot a wooden stake in half wins; or the Mike Fink shoot, where the object is to blast an artist's conception of a tin cup off an artist's conception of a pilgrim's head with a pistol. If you hit the cup drawn on the target instead of the pilgrim, in theory it would have flown off his head. And, naturally, there are tomahawk and knife throws, fire-starting contests with flint and steel, and even an occasional cook-off with ancient recipes.

Not quite as abruptly as the day began, but still suddenly enough to take you by surprise, the bustle of activity winds down. Evening turns to night. The rowdies have gone off to tip over an outhouse with some unfortunate soul enthroned therein. You might hear them across the way, like a bunch of yelping coyotes in the far, far distance. Conversations in hushed tones fade in and out of earshot. Campfires, once blazing, now glow with that satisfying, deep orange. Candle lanterns by the dozen flicker in random pattern across the camp, like Japanese lamps over the patio when a party has ended.

It's a bit lonely—yet it's beautiful.

APPENDIX A
DIRECTORY OF BLACK POWDER TRADE

FIREARMS

ALLEN FIREARMS MANUFACTURING
1107 Penn Road
Santa Fe, NM 87501
(Imports Italian-made revolvers, rifles)

THE ARMOURY, INC.
Route 202
New Preston, CT 06777
(Imports muzzleloading guns)

ARMSPORT, INC.
3590 NW 49th Street
Miami, FL 33142
(Imports revolvers, pistols, rifles, & shotguns from Italy)

FRANK BARTLETT
Route 4, Box 255
Gallatin, TN 37066
(Hand-crafted custom rifles)

JOHN BERGMAN
Rural Route 1
Paris, TN 38242
(Custom-crafted muzzleloading guns)

M. BRITT
201 Islandia Drive
Placenta, CA 92670
(Custom rifles)

CONNECTICUT VALLEY ARMS
5988 Peach Tree Corners East
Norcross, GA 30092
(Imports black-powder guns from Spain)

DIXIE GUN WORKS
Gunpowder Lane
Union City, TN 38261
(Imports muzzleloading guns & supplies antique parts)

EuroArms OF AMERICA
P.O. Box 3277
Winchester, VA 22601
(Imports British Enfields)

LEROY FLEANOR
Route 16, Box 204
Grey, TN 37615
(Custom rifles)

GARRETT ARMS & IMPORTS
24 Southern Shopping Center
Norfolk, VA 23505
(Imports Italian muzzleloading guns)

KASSNAR IMPORTS, INC.
5480 Linglestown Road
Harrisburg, PA 17110
(Imports left-handed Hawken rifles)

LYMAN PRODUCTS CORP.
Route 147
Middlefield, CT 06455
(Imports Great Plains rifle)

NAVY ARMS
689 Bergen Blvd.
Ridgefield, NJ 07657
(Imports reproduction guns)

SPRINGFIELD FIREARMS CORP.
604 Cottage St.
Springfield, MA 01104
(Copy of Colt 1861 rifled musket)

STURM, RUGER & CO.
Lacey Place
Southport, CT 06490
(Ruger Old Army .44-caliber revolvers)

THOMPSON/CENTER ARMS
Farmington Road
Rochester, NH 03867
(American-made muzzleloading guns)

BLACK POWDER ACCESSORIES

AMERICANA, LTD.
3902 Spring Hill Road
Louisville, KY 40207
(Replica 1850 knife blades)

ATLANTA CUTLERY
P.O. Box 839
Conyers, GA 30207
(Green River pattern knives)

E.C. BISHOP & SONS, INC.
P.O. Box 7
Warsaw, MO 65355
(Replacement stocks for black-powder rifles)

BLUE STAR TIPIS
P.O. Box 2562-E
Missoula, MT 59806
(Authentic Sioux, Cheyenne, Crow, & Blackfeet tepees)

E. CHRISTOPHER FIREARMS CO.
8007 State Route 128
Miamitown, OH 45041
(Replica eighteenth and nineteenth century knife blades)

CRAZY CROW TRADING POST
Box 314-6
Denison, TX 75020
(Supplies for modern mountain men)

EARTHWORKS TIPIS
P.O. Box 28
Ridway, CO 81432
(Replicas of western plains tepees)

GREY OWL INDIAN CRAFT CO.
113-15 Springfield Blvd.
Queens Village, NY 11429
(Beads, trade silver)

KOLPIN INC.
P.O. Box 231
Berlin, WI 54923
(Leather cases for muzzleloading rifles)

LEE PRECISION, INC.
4275 Highway U
Hartford, WI 53027
(Round balls for front-loading guns)

OCTOBER COUNTRY
P.O. Box 1206-L
Post Falls, ID 83854
(Leather shooting bags and powder horns)

RENEGADE HUNTING RANGE
P.O. Box 741
Crossville, TN 38555
(Muzzleloading wild boar hunts)

UPPER MISSOURI TRADING CO.
Box 191
Crofton, NE 68730
(Accessories for black-powder shooters)

ORGANIZATIONS

BRIGADE OF THE AMERICAN REVOLUTION
32 Douglas Road
Delmar, NY 12054

INTERNATIONAL BLACK POWDER
HUNTING ASSOCIATION
P.O. Box 1180
Glenrock, WY 82637

NATIONAL MUZZLELOADING
RIFLE ASSOCIATION
Box 67
Friendship, IN 47021

NORTH/SOUTH SKIRMISH ASSOCIATION
9700 Royerton Drive
Richmond, VA 23228

PUBLICATIONS

BLACK POWDER HUNTING
P.O. Box 1180
Glenrock, WY 82637

BLACK POWDER TIMES
P.O. Box 842
Mount Vernon, WA 98273

MUZZLEBLASTS
Box 67
Friendship, IN 47021

MUZZLELOADER
Route 5, Box 347-M
Texarkana, TX 75501

SKIRMISH LINE
P.O. Box 363
Moorestown, NJ 08057

SMOKE AND FIRE NEWS
P.O. Box 166
Grand Rapids, OH 43522

THE TOMAHAWK & LONG RIFLE
16630 Penny Avenue
Sandlake, MI 49343

BUCKSKINNING MERCHANTS

AVALON FORGE
409 Gun Road
Baltimore, MD 21227

BITTERROOT TRADING POST
910 North First Street
Hamilton, MT 59840

BLUE EYES SHOOTS COMPANY
1809 Ravenwood Drive
Concord, CA 94520

BUCKSKIN SUPPLY COMPANY
Box B
Cherokee, TX 76832

THE BUFFALO BULL
Box 8
Marion, IA 52302

BUFFALO HOOF TRADING COMPANY
Box 103
Gowrie, IA 50543

CRAZY CROW
107 North Fannin
Denison, TX 75020

FORT GREENVILLE TRADING COMPANY
2 Front Drive
Little Hocking, OH 45742

FRENCH LICK TRADING COMPANY
Box 825
Gallatin, TN 37066

GOLDEN AGE ARMS
Box 283
Delaware, OH 43015

GREY OWL INDIAN CRAFT COMPANY
113-15 Springfield Bloulevard
Queens Village, NY 11429

INDIAN RIDGE TRADERS
Box 869
Royal Oak, MI 48068

LOG CABIN SHOP
Box 275
Lodi, OH 44254

LOU'S LEATHERS
Route 1, Box 176-A
Elk Horn, KY 42733

MEDICINE MOUNTAIN TRADING COMPANY
Box 124
Sturgis, SD 55785

MOCCASIN HEAVEN
112 East Kossuth
Columbus, OH 43206

WAHKON BAY COMPANY
Route 1, Box 101 B
Wahkon, MN 56386

NORTHWEST OUTPOST
520 South Hayes
Moscow, ID 83840

NORTHWEST TRADERS
4999 Packard Drive
Dayton, OH 45424

SALISH HOUSE
Box 27
Rollins, MT 59931

TECUMSEH'S TRADING POST
Box 369
Sharlesville, PA 19554

TRAPPERS RENDEZVOUS
Box 8822
Denver, CO 80201

UPPER MISSOURI TRADING COMPANY
Box 191
Crofton, NE 68730

APPENDIX B
RENDEZVOUS AND SHOOT DATES

ALABAMA

WHITE WATER LONGHUNTERS
Shoot: last Sunday of month
February-October
James R. Swift
210 Cherry Hill Road
Enterprise, AL 36330

ALASKA

McKINLEY MOUNTAIN MEN
Rifle and pistol shoot: second Sunday each month
Shotgun shoot: fourth Saturday each month
Ray Tomory
HC 78, Box 3587
Chugiak, AK 99567

MIDNIGHT SUN MUZZLELOADERS
Shoot: every other Sunday
Dave Nester
P.O. Box 10612
Fairbanks, AK 99710

MUSKEG MUZZLELOADERS CLUB
Shoot: second Sunday each month
P.O. Box 34756
Juneau, AK 99803

ARIZONA

AZ CACTUS CAPPERS M.L.G.C.
Shoot: third Sunday each month
Chuck Zufall
7322 North 20th Drive
Phoenix, AZ. 85021

BUCKSKINNERS
Shoot: third Sunday each month
Lane Brown
P.O. Box 397
Williams, AZ 86046

MAZATZAL MOUNTAIN M.L.
Shoot: second Saturday each month
Peter R. Waichulaitus
137 East Jasmine Street
Mesa, AZ 85201

MONTEZUMA MUZZLE LOADERS
Shoot: twice each month
C.E. Furlong
P.O. Box 605
Sierra Vista, AZ 85636

OLD PUEBLO MUZZLE LOADERS
Fun shoot: second Sunday each month
Aggregate shoot: fourth Sunday each month
Lina Kaas
6942 West Flying W
Tucson, AZ 85746

THE POWDERHORN CLAN
Primitive rendezvous and shoots
sites and dates vary monthly
Dale Shadle
P.O. Box 1464
Snowflake, AZ 85937

WALAPAI MOUNTAIN MUZZLE LOADERS
Shoot: second weekend each month
Ed Haywood
P.O. Box 6483
Kingman, AZ 86402

YUMA TERRITORIAL LONG RIFLES
Shoot: last Sunday each month
Yuma Leather Plus
Attn: Richard Dupree
1020 South Fourth Avenue, # 2
Yuma, AZ 85364

ARKANSAS

ARKANSAS MUZZLE LOADING ASSOCIATION
Robert W. Wiley
Route 5, Box 270
Monticello, AR 71655

FOOTHILLS MUZZLE LOADERS
Shoot: second Sunday each month
Twin Lakes Gun Club
John McKinney
P.O. Box 199
Mountain Home, AR 72653

CALIFORNIA

THE AMERICAN MOUNTAIN MEN
Shoot: second week of July and assorted week-
ends during year
Terry Avery
16630 Penny Avenue
Sandlake, MI 49343

AMERICAN RIVER MUZZLE LOADERS
Shoot: first Sunday each month
Phil Coleman
5708 Sutter Avenue
Carmichael, CA 95608

BIG HORN MOUNTAIN MEN
Shoot: second Sunday each month.
Chris Dias
P.O. Box 1275
Fontana, CA 92334

BRUSHY CREEK RANGERS
Shoot: Sunday after third Thursday each month
Clara Lambert
1099 Grand Avenue
Marysville, CA 95961

BURBANK MUZZLE LOADERS
Shoot: second Sunday each month
Black powder muzzleloader and cartridge silhou-
ette matches fourth Sunday each month
Thomas Trevor
11552 Swinton Avenue
Grenada Hills, CA 91334

COYOTE CREEK MUZZLE LOADERS
Shoot: first Sunday each month
Allen Schneck
36248 Worthing Drive
Newark, CA 94560

DESERT MARKSMEN RIFLE & PISTOL CLUB
B.P. SECTION
Fun shoot: third Sunday each month
Dave Bell
38551 Dunmore
Palmdale, CA 93550

DIABLO BUCKSKINNERS, INC.
Monthly shoots: first and third Saturday
Francis Morris
P.O. Box 5266
Hercules, CA 94547

FLINTLOCK ERA ASSOCIATION AND SOCIETY
Shoot: fourth Sunday each month
Mart Ott
2538 Highway 99
Biggs, CA 95917

FORT SUTTER MUZZLE LOADERS
Primitive shoot: second Sunday each month
Formal shoot: fourth Sunday each month
Ed Jones
4208 Lantana Avenue
Sacramento, CA 95824

FRESNO MUZZLE LOADERS
Offhand matches: first Sunday each month
Shotgun matches: third Sunday each month
Joe Walker Rendezvous—October
Greydon Hicks
(209) 299-4429

GOLDEN EAGLE MOUNTAIN MEN
Shoot: first weekend each month
14932 Dorothy Place
Victorville, CA 92329

LOMPAC MUZZLELOADERS
Shoot: third Sunday each month
Rich and Betty Ralph
4051 Polaris Avenue
Lompoc, CA 93436

MATURANGO MUZZLELOADERS
Shoot: third Saturday each month
Peggy L. Wandell
P.O. Box 1084
Inyokern, CA 93527

MOUNTAIN RANCH MUZZLE LOADERS, INC.
Shoot: first and third Sunday each month at Taylor Park in railroad flat.
Pat Wescombe
P.O. Box 488
Glenco, CA 95232

OJAI VALLEY MUZZLE LOADERS
Shoot: third weekend each month
Bill Bland
4510 Justin Way
Oxnard, CA 93033

SAN DIEGO COUNTY MUZZLE LOADERS
Shoot: first Sunday each month
Dennis Sherman
10121 Calle Marinero
Spring Valley, CA 92077

SIERRA MUZZLE LOADERS
Shoot: first Sunday each month
Ava Baker
P.O. Box 112
Browns Valley, CA 95918

SMOKEY VALLEY MUZZLE LOADERS
Shoot: third Sunday each month
413 Pepper Tree Drive
Brea, CA 92621

SOLANO MUZZLE LOADERS ASSOCIATION
Shoot: first Sunday and third Saturday each month
Carolyn Rosal
1025 Taylor Avenue
Vallejo, CA 94591

SOUTHWEST FREETRAPPERS ASSOCIATION
Shoot: third Sunday each month
Allen Jennings
9100 Arcadia, #30
Fontana, CA 92335

STONY CREEK MUZZLE LOADERS
Shoot: third Saturday each month
James E. Blakeman
312 8th Street
Orland, CA 95963

COLORADO

BIJOU BASIN FREE TRAPPERS
Shoot: second Sunday each month
Steven Dreiling
2221 Moccasin Drive
Colorado Springs, CO 80915

COLORADO SPRINGS MUZZLE LOADERS, INC.
Shotgun shoot: first Sunday each month
Primitive shoot: third Sunday monthly
George Bennett
1909 Meyers Avenue
Colorado Springs, CO 80909

FORT WICKED MUZZLE LOADERS
Blanket and prize shoot: fourth Sunday each month
(303) 522-4281

GRAND MESA MUZZLELOADERS
Shoot: last Sunday each month
Del Behring
(303) 434-9594

MONTROSE MOUNTAIN MEN
Shoot: second Sunday each month
Ron Rock
(303) 249-7188

UTE TRAIL MUZZLELOADERS
Shoot: last Sunday each month
P.O. Box 4597
Woodland Park, CO 80866

WEST ELK MOUNTAIN MEN
Shoot: second Sunday each month
Diana Keune
P.O.Box 56
Paonai, CO 81428

CONNECTICUT

BLACK POWDER SPORTSMAN SOCIETY
Annual shoot: October
Sharon Leiber
17 Watch Hill Dr.
Cromwell, CT 06416

LIBERTY HILL MUZZLELOADERS
Edmond Leet
RFD #2, Tobacco Street
Lebanon, CT 06249

MEDAD HILLS M.L. GUN CLUB
Shoot: first and third Sunday each month
Joe Sacca
(203) 354-0725

PACHAUG LONG RIFLES M.L.B.P.C.
Shoot: second Sunday each month
Thomas F. Brown
30 Westminster Road
Baltic, CT 06330

PATTAGUASSETT MUZZLELOADERS
Turkey shoot: October
Christmas blanket shoot: December
Howard Barron
26 Oakwood Drive
Madison, CT 06443

QUOKETAUG RANGERS
Shoot: last Sunday each month
Albert F. Sousa
429 Buddington Road
Groton, CT 06340

DELAWARE

BRANDYWINE LONG RIFLES
State championships: September
Turkey shoot: November
Handgun shoot: December
Tim Gerrish
2647 Abington Road
Wilmington, DE 19810

FLORIDA

CALUSA COUNTRY LONG RIFLES
Shoot: fourth Sunday each month
Port Malabar Rifle and Pistol Range
Bob Hall
571 Duval Street, NE
Palm Bay, FL 32927

CENTRAL FLORIDA RIFLE & PISTOL CLUB, INC.
Matches third Sunday each month
Richard Graffuis
(407) 896-6793

ESCAMBIA RIVER M.L.
Shoots first and third Sunday each month
Rendezvous: November
Brenda Rayburn
10020 N. Pensacola Boulevard
Pensacola, FL 32534

EVERGLADES CAP & BALL BLACK POWDER
HISTORICAL SHOOTING ASSOCIATION
Shoot: second Sunday each month
Phil Schmidt
631 North 66 Terrace
Hollywood, FL 33024

EVERGLADES RIFLE & PISTOL CLUB
Shoot: first Sunday each month
Tom Seren
(407) 969-2738

FLORIDA FRONTIERSMEN
Shoot: first Sunday each month
Alafia River Rendezvous: each January
Ron Clark
P.O. Box 66736
St. Petersburg, FL 33736

HIGHLANDS GUN CLUB
Shoot: second Sunday each month
Ron Sproule
(813) 385-4478

TREATY OAK LONGRIFLES
Shoot: fourth Sunday each month
Steven Crider
1977 Muncie Avenue
Jax, FL 32210

GEORGIA

BEAR CREEK MUZZLELOADERS
Rendezvous: November
Betty Powell
7695 Atlanta Newnan Road
Palmetto, GA 30268

BLUE RIDGE MOUNTAIN MEN, INC.
Shoot: fourth weekend each month except
November and December
John Harkins
Box 1514, Route 1
Demorest, GA 30535

BRUSHY CREEK MUZZLELOADERS
Shoot: fourth Sunday each month
Sam Pair
2225 Meadowbrook Drive
Tifton, GA 31794

CHEROKEE BARK BUSTERS
Shoot: first Sunday each month
Robert Bennett
83 Brookshire Drive
Carrollton, GA 30117

FLINT RIVER LONG RIFLES
Shoot: second Sunday each month
P.O. Box 70612
Albany, GA 31707

KIOKEE RIFLES
Elija Clark Rifle Frolic, a primitive rendezvous:
October
Dot "Short" Shields
P.O. Box 524
Thompson, GA 30824

LITTLE RIVER MUZZLELOADERS
Shoot: second Sunday each month
P.O. Box 2342
Moultrie, GA 31776

MUSCOGEE LONG RIFLES
Shoot: second Sunday each month
Curt Stables
517 Harris Circle
Ft. Benning, GA. 31905

SOUTHERN SHOOTING
HERITAGE ASSOCIATION
Shoot: third Sunday each month
Jon Pendergrass
1201 Redland Court
Lawrenceville, GA 30245

TRAIL OF TEARS LONG RIFLES
Shoot: first Sunday each month
John Adcock
(912) 453-8007

IDAHO

COEUR D'ALENE MUZZLELOADERS
Shoot: fourth Sunday each month
Jane M. Stoll
5530 Cloverleaf Road
Hauser Lake, ID 83854

EE-DA-HOW LONG RIFLES
Shoot: third Sunday each month
Chuck Chaney
(208) 345-6360

PORT NEUF MUZZLE LOADERS, INC.
Shoot: third Sunday each month
Thomas Yadon
4928 Pleasant View
Pocatello, ID 83202

ILLINOIS

BEAR CREEK PRIMITIVE MT. MEN.
Shoot: third weekend each month
Jean Beard
Box 542
Kincaid, IL 62540

CRAWFORD COUNTY B.P. CLUB
Regular shoots first full weekend every month
Grace Carrico
RR 1, Box 281
Odon, IN 47562

FT. DEARBORN FRONTIERSMEN
Shoot: third Sunday each month
Larry Akers
835 Charles Street
Aurora, IL 60506

GOSHEN TRAIL LONGRIFLES
Kevin Settle
(618) 242-7931

ILLINI MUZZLELOADERS, INC.
Cash shoot: September
Turkey shoot: October
Jim Sellers
5612 West Sioux Trail
Peoria, IL 61607

ILLINOIS STATE RIFLE ASSOCIATION
Cash shoot: third Sunday each month
Fall Rendezvoud: October
Turkey shoot: November
Winter Rendezvous: February
Randy Hedden
(815) 723-4759

JOLIET MUZZLE LOADERS
Shoot: second Sunday each month
Rendezvous: October
Dave Lyons
Box 392
Minooka, IL 60447

LEROY RIFLE & PISTOL CLUB
Monthly shoots
Jim Nalley
(309) 663-2749

OKAW VALLEY MUZZLE LOADERS
Shoot: first Sunday each month
Linda Miller
RR 2, Box 179
Tower Hill, IL 62571

PRAIRIELAND FRONTIERSMEN, INC.
Shoot: second Sunday each month
Camp and Shoot: October
Turkey shoot: November
Camp and Shoot: February
Steven K. Wood
P.O. Box 195
Sullivan, IL 61951

ROCK RUN LONG RIFLES
Shoot: first Sunday each month
Fall rendezvous and shoot: October
Paul Swanson
(815) 248-2405

SHILOH VALLEY MUZZLE LOADERS
Shoot: third Sunday each month
Max Burkhart
(618) 337-9073

WOLF RIDGE MUZZLELOADERS
Fall rendezvous: October
"Mule" Brand
(217) 839-4025

INDIANA

BLUE RIVER LONGRIFLES, INC.
Powder and cap shoot: September
Mike Cochran
348 North Bazil Avenue
Indianapolis, IN 46219

BREWER HOLLOW LONG RIFLES INC.
Meat shoot: September
Fall rendezvous: October
David Smoke
(812) 279-4258

BUCK CREEK MUZZLELOADERS
Labor Day rifle frolic
Turkey shoot: November
David O'Bryan
RR 3, Box 151
Linton, IN 47441

CONNER PRAIRIE RIFLES
Wm. Conner Traditional Shoot: October
John Weston
P.O. Box 3
Fishers, IN 46038

FALL CREEK VALLEY CONSERVATION CLUB
Grocery shoot: September and October
Frederick Peterson
Route 1, Box 94 B
Yorktown, IN 47396

FALLS OF THE OHIO MUZZLE LOADERS
Monthly shoots: third Sunday
Dennis M. Harrison
8110 Autumn Drive
Georgetown, IN 47122

FISH CREEK LONGRIFLES
Turkey shoot: November
Christmas shoot: December
Pam Canellas
Route 1, Box 115
Butlerville, IN 47223

FORT TASSINONG MUZZLELOADERS, INC.
Shoot: second Sunday each month
Kathy Sebben
12504 Clark Street
Crown Point, IN 46307

FT. WAYNE RIFLE & REVOLVER CLUB
Shoot: first Sunday each month
Jim Hoelle
(219) 484-5755

KEKIONGA LONGRIFLES
Kristine Maritin
2107-2C Point West Drive
Fort Wayne, IN 46808

LAUGHERY VALLEY MUZZLELOADERS
Shoot: second Sunday each month
Margie Kreimer
5220 Zion Road
Cleves, OH 45002

LEWIS & CLARK MUZZLELOADERS
Fun shoot: third Saturday each month
David L. Metzger
2316 Crums Lane
Jeffersonville, IN 47130

MAHAWA SIPIWI M.L.
Pistol and shotgun shoot: October
Turkey shoot: October
Charles E. Hodges
1019 Northfield Drive
Lebanon, IN 46052

MARSHALL COUNTY LONGRIFLES
Shoot: first Sunday each month
Wm. Rechtenbaugh
17780 W. 6th Road
Plymouth, IN 46563

MICHIGAN CITY RIFLE CLUB
Open shoot: first Sunday each month
Ray Clemens
425 Firefly Drive
Michigan City, IN 46360

MORGAN COUNTY LONGRIFLES
Merchandise shoot: September
Fall rendezvous: October
Turkey shoot: November
Ham shoot: December
Blanket shoot: January
Lori Boroff
8959 North Lewis Lane
Bloomington, IN 47408

OUABACHE LONGRIFLES
Meat shoot: second Saturday each month
Greg Spaulding
0359 South 200 West
Bluffton, IN 46714

PATOKA VALLEY LONGRIFLES, INC.
Turkey shoot: October
Woods walk: December
Joe Schnapf
2888 Terri Lane
Newburgh, IN 47630

PEQUANNAH M.L. CLUB
Meat and turkey shoot: November
Bean pot shoot: December
Carol Drew
601 Glen Ellen Drive
Union City, IN 47390

PIGEON ROOST M.L.
Shoot: second Sunday each month
David W. Baker
Box 53 North Elm Street
Medora, IN 47260

PLAINSMEN MUZZLELOADING CLUB
Shoot: third Sunday each month
Sandra Perry
1349 C.R. 27
Waterloo, IN 46793

RIVER VALLEY MUZZLELOADERS
Shoot: third Sunday each month
Beth Chubb
1803 East Warren Woods
Buchanan, MI 49107

SAND DUNES LONG RIFLES
Shoot: first Sunday each month
Ron Wyller
2560 Orange
Lake Station, IN 46405

SNAKE HOLLER MUZZLELOADERS
Shoot: second Sunday each month
Sheila Adams
RR 1
Dana, IN 47847

STONES TRACE REGULATORS
Shoot: second Sunday each month
Rendezvous: September
Brad L. Smith
Route 2, Box 64
Syracuse, IN 46567

THUMPERKEG LONGRIFLES INC.
Open shoot: first Sunday each month
B.J. Lewis
3011 Edgewood Drive
Evansville, IN 47712

THUNDER CREEK LONGRIFLES, INC.
Shoot: third Sunday each month
Glen McLain
Route 2
Morgantown, IN 46160

TRI-COUNTY COONHUNTER'S M.L.
Shoot: third Sunday each month
Bertha Hazelwood
RR 1, Box 219
Batesville, IN 47006

TWIN RIVERS MUZZLELOADERS
Shoot: first Sunday after first Wednesday each
month
Terry L. Young
RR 4, Box 172
Winamac, IN 46996

WAHPANIPE M.L.C.
Offhand shoot: October
Over-the-Log shoot: October
Allen Coon
(317) 679-5408

WETZEL TRACE LONG RIFLES
Two-day shoot: September
Deer hunters shoot: October
Ron Borron
302 Village Road
Bargersville, IN 46106

WILDCAT VALLEY M.L. CLUB, INC.
Turkey and meat: November
Robert Ehman
1004 Tepee Drive
Kokomo, IN 46902

IOWA

SIOUX RIVER MUZZLELOADERS
Shoot: third Sunday each month
Rich Bishop
1316 29th Street
Sioux City, IA 51104

KANSAS

CAPITOL CITY GUN CLUB, INC.
Emmett Conner
(913) 267-2345

CHIEF BLACK DOG'S TRAIL M.L. CLUB
Fall family rendezvous: October
Ted Sprague
Route 1, Box 150
Oswego, KS 67356

FIRST SANTA FE TRAIL PLAINSMEN
Shoot: third Sunday each month
Duane Collins
211 Rice Road
Topeka, KS 66607

JEDEDIAH SMITH MUZZLELOADERS
Shoot: third Sunday each month
Rendezvous: September
Dennis E. Burk
RR 1, Box 8 A
Spearville, KS 67876

REPUBLICAN VALLEY M.L.
Shoot: first Saturday each month
Dan Long
Box 26
Leonardville, KS 66449

SWAN RIVER MUZZLELOADERS
Shoot: second Sunday each month
Rose M. Feeback
1101 Pacific
Osawatomic, KS 66064

KENTUCKY

AURORA BLACKPOWDER
Fall rendezvous: third weekend October
Richard and Peggy Keiper
P.O. Box 1473
Boyd, TX 76023

BREATHITT CTY. L.R. ASSOC., INC.
Shoot: third Sunday each month
Don Combs
P.O. Box 391
Jackson, KY 41339

BRYAN STATION M.L.
Shoot: fourth Sunday each month
Barry Cecil
1420 Mout Rainer Drive
Lexington, KY 40517

BUCK SPORT LONGHUNTERS
Shoot: second Sunday each month
Gary Powell
2086 Hodgenville Road
Elizabethtown, KY 42701

COL. FLEMING MUZZLE LOADERS, INC.
Shoot: second Sunday each month
Bill Rawlings
Route 3, 204 Emmons Lane
Flemingsburg, KY 41041

KENTUCKY CORPS OF LONGRIFLEMEN, INC.
Annual team shoot: October
Jeff Talbert
4506 Valley View Lane
Taylor Mill, KY 41015

LONG RIFLES OF THE DARK HUNTING GROUND
Fun shoot: third Sunday each month
Wilson Guynn III
225 Spring Lake
Madisonville, KY 42431

NELSON COUNTY M.L. CLUB
Shoot: first Sunday each month
115 Blue Grass Court
Bardstown, KY 40004

OLE' CAINTUCKEE PRIMITIVES
Shoot: fourth weekend each month
Shelly Jacob
6804 Sebree Drive #6
Florence, KY 41042

STUMP BLUFF MILITIA
Fall rendezvous: September
William Blondin
3206 Mount Lebanon Road
Alvaton, KY 42122

LOUISIANA

FUSELIERS OF THE SWAMP
State shoot: September
Turkey shoot: November
William Hornsey
18750 Old Scenic Highway, Lot 24
Zachary, LA 70791

MAINE

THE ANCIENT ONES
Fort Barlow shoot: October
RR 1, Box 2430
Anson, ME 04911

PENOBSCOT LONGRIFLES M.L.
Shoot: last Sunday each month
Colby Moon
(207) 487-2730

SOMERSET COUNTY MUZZLELOADERS
Chicken shoot: September
Ham shoot: October
Blanket shoot: October
George Mullin
Route. 1, Box 2320
North Anson, ME 04958

MARYLAND

CHOPTANK M.L. ASSOCIATION
Silhouette shoot: October
Turkey shoot: November and December
Chuck Pittinger
Route 2, Box 75
Denton, MD 21629

MARRIOTSVILLE M.L., INC.
Beef shoot: September
David Scanlan
318 Oella Avenue
Cantonsville, MD. 21228

MINERAL CO. WESTERN MARYLAND. M.L.
Club Championship: September
Fred Kreiger
13807 Brart Avenue
Cresaptown, MD 21502

PATCH & BALL M.L. ASSOC.
Charles D. Dicken Sr.
38 Locust Street
LaVale, MD 21502

TIDEWATER MUZZLELOADERS, INC.
5-X Beef shoot: October
Pistol shoot: November
Turkey shoot: December
Joe Cashwell
4610 Sargent Road NE
Washington, DC 20017

MASSACHUSETTS

APPONAGANSETT VOLUNTEER RIFLES
Fall Shoot: September
Ron Plourde
483 Old Westport Road
NoRTH Dartmouth, MA 02747

BARRE SPORTSMANS CLUB -
"MICHEWAUG MUZZLE LOADERS"
Turkey shoot: October
William Perkins
Route 1, Box 63, Old Barre Road
Barre, MA 01005

TAUNTON RIFLE & PISTOL CLUB, INC.
William L. Cronan
715 Cohannet Street
Taunton, MA 02780

WACHUSETT MOUNTAIN MEN
Shoot: every Sunday
Gregson Cobb
32 Main Boulevard
Shrewsbury, MA 01545

MICHIGAN

ALPENA MUZZLE LOADERS
Shoot: third Sunday each month
R.J. Bordeau
P.O. Box 881
Alpena, MI 49707

ATTICA MUZZLELOADERS CLUB
Marvin Davis
2410 Jossman Road
Holly, MI 48442

THE BENZIE SPORTSMEN'S CLUB
Shoot: every Tuesday from November to May
Turkey shoot: October
Don Collins
(616) 882- 5181

BLUE WATER SPORTSMEN
Shoot: every Tuesday from May to September
Turkey shoot: October
Homer Melat
(313) 325-1422

BOLLING WATER M.L.
Shoot: second Wednesday from May to August
Fall shoot: September
J.S. Wolbers
3731 Greenleaf Circle, Apt. 308
Kalamazoo, MI 49008

CLINTON RIVER MUZZLELOADERS
Primitive blanket shoot: third Sunday each month
Rendezvous: October
Winterfest : February
Bill Smith
21120 Erben
St. Clair Shores, MI 48081

COLUMBIAVILLE SPORTSMENS CLUB, INC.
Shoot: third Sunday each month
Turkey shoot: October
Wesley C. O'Dell
217 West Burnside Street
Caro, MI 48723

GRAND VALLEY CAP "N" BALLERS
Shoot: first Sunday each month
Jim Galiger
P.O. Box 99
Allegan, MI 49010

HOUGHTON LAKE MUZZLELOADERS
Woods walk: October
Eli (Sam) Cogar
P.O. Box 755
Houghton Lake, MI 48629

HOWARD CITY CONSERVATION CLUB
Shoot: second Sunday each month
Jane Salo
15853 Cottonwood, Lot #11
Cedar Springs, MI 49139

LANSING M.L. GUN CLUB
Shoot: second Sunday each month
Sheila Heiser
311 Berry Street
Lansing, MI 48910

THE LONG RIFLES OF THE HART
Shoot: second Sunday and fourth Thursday from
April to August
Lori Davis
Route 1, 88th Avenue
Pentwater, MI 49449

MANISTEE CLAN M.L., INC.
Shoot: first and third Sunday each month
Harry Foster
390 Second Street
Manistee, MI 49660

MASSASAUGA VALLEY M.L.
Shoot: second and fourth Sunday each month
William H. Gale
946 State Road
Quincy, MI 49082

MICHIGAN STATE M.L. ASSOC.
Woods walk: October
Allan Pichon
24810 Woodland
Flat Rock, MI 48134

MICHIGAN SCHUETZEN SOCIETY
John Grant
1330 House Road
Webberville, MI 48892

NEW OCEA FREE TRAPPERS
Shoot: second Sunday each month
David G. Noble
441 Apache Drive
Fremont, MI 49412

RICHFIELD RIFLES
Jack Redmond
11425 Carr Road
Davison, MI 48423

SAGINAW FIELD & STREAM CLUB
Shoot: last Tuesday each month
Jim De Clerck
1481 Timothy
Saginaw, MI 48603

SAUK TRAIL LONG RIFLES
Shoot: second Sunday each month
Turkey shoot: October
Hog rendezvous: February
Ken Stuck
9 McCollum
Hillsdale, MI 49242

WASHTENAW PIONEER M.L.
Founders shoot: September
Hunters shoot: October
Turkey shoot: November
Holiday shoot: December
Dick or Carol Potts
9551 Stark Road
Livonia, MI 48150

WESTERN WAYNE COUNTY
CONSERVATION ASSOC.
Shoot: second Sunday each month
Fall rendezvous: Labor day weekend
Elizabeth Darnell
45096 Geddes
Canton, MI 48188

MINNESOTA
LOOKOUT MT. B.P. SOCIETY
Shoot: first Saturday each month
Charley Red Sky
819 7th St. South
Virginia, MN 55792

NORTH STAR FREE TRAPPERS
Shoot: monthly
Rendezvous: September
Ken (Grizz) Yazek
5222 Dewes Road North
Brainerd, MN 56401

MISSISSIPPI

HATCHIE RUN SMOKEPOLES
Shoot: fourth Sunday each month
Joyce E. Smith
P.O. Box 1175
Corinth, MS 38834

MAGNOLIA M.L. ASSOCIATION
Shoot: first Sunday each month
Walter M. Mabry
2102 Plantation Boulevard
Jackson, MS 39211-2812

NATCHEZ FREE TRAPPERS
Shoot: second Sunday each month
Matt Avance
118 South Canal Street
Natchez, MS 39120

TOMBIGBEE VALLEY M.L.
Shoot: third Sunday each month
Don Morgan
(601) 844-4757

MISSOURI

BALDRIDGE FREE TRAPPERS
Shoot: first Sunday each month
John E. Stapleton
RR 2
Fayette, MO 65248

BULL CREEK MOUNTAIN BOOMERS
Shoot: first Sunday each month
Rick Wyman
P.O. Box 1244
Forsyth, MO 65633

CREEDMOOR RIFLE CLUB
Shoot: fourth Sunday each month
Barry Munsell
801 Love Drive
O'Fallon, MO 63366

CROOKED RIVER BASIN M.L.
Shoot: first Sunday each month
Kathy Goodale
Route 2, Box 152A
Rayville, MO 64084

FORT HILL RAMRODS
Rendezvous: September
Frank Logsden
(314) 375-3891

GEMMER MUZZLELOADING CLUB
State Silhouette shoot: September
Turkey shoot: November
Buffalo shoot: December
Steven M. Kestle
1816 LaSalle Street
St. Louis, MO 63104

GRAND RIVER MUZZLELOADERS
Lost Creek rendezvous: September
Cindy Asher
(816) 632-6048

OSAGE TRACE FREE TRAPPERS, INC.
Shoot: October
Dianne Prock
Route 1, Box 28A
Falcon, MO 65470

OZARK MOUNTAIN LONGRIFLES
Fall rendezvous: October
Jack Steelman
H.C. Route, Box 64A
Hartshorn, MO 65479

OZARK MOUNTAIN M.L.
Shoot: third Sunday each month
Elaine Crabtree
429 W. Woodridge
Springfield, MO 65803

STROTHER FREETRAPPERS B.P. CLUB
Cindy Matteson
1202 A. E. Third Street Terr.
Lee's Summit, MO 64063

THE TRAPPERS OF STARVED ROCK
Rendezvous: October
Mel Warnoff
1529 Sherman Drive
St. Charles, MO 63301

MONTANA

BEARTOOTH MOUNTAINMEN
Shoot: September
Tony Wayland
10 Lincoln Road West
Helena, MT 59601

BRIDGER MOUNTAIN MEN
Shoot: third weekend each month
Darlene Stuart
301 Quaw Boulevard
Belgrade, MT 59714

BUFFALO ROAD MUZZLELOADERS
Shoot: third weekend each month
John Osterman
1513 Easy Street
Butte, MT 59701

ELK RIVER PLAINSMEN
Shoot: fourth Sunday each month
Bob Goldsberry
(406) 259-6253

LITTLE BIGHORN MOUNTAIN MEN
Regular shoot: September and Ocotber
Turkey shoot : November
Santa Claus shoot: December
Debbie "Cottontop" Stoddard
P.O. Box 254
Hardin, MT 59034

LOWER YELLOWSTONE PLAINSMEN
Shoot: September
Carolyn Huber
Box 362
Terry , MT 59349

NEBRASKA

FORT ATKINSON M.L., INC.
Fall shoot: October
James E. Potter
Route 6
Lincoln, NE 68502

NEBRASKA MUZZLELOADING
RIFLE ASSOCIATION
State shoot: September
Turkey shoot: October
Jack L. Miller
P.O. Box 241
Grand Island, NE 68801

NEVADA

HUMBOLDT RIVER M.L.
Shoot: last Saturday each month
Marie White
875½ 2nd Street
Elko, NV 89801

NEW JERSEY

QUINTON SPORTSMAN'S CLUB, INC.
Shoot: first and third Sunday each month
Blanket shoot: September
Coon shoot: September
Turkey shoot: November
Duck shoot: December
Johnathan Sparks
(609) 935-7014

NEW MEXICO

NEW MEXICO BIG HORN GUN CLUB
Shoot: second Sunday each month
c/o High Point Gun Shop
S.R. Box 98
Tijeras, NM 87059

NEW YORK

ADIRONDACK LONG RIFLES, INC.
Marilyn Lahah
105 1st Street
Boonville, NY 13309

ALABAMA M.L. HUNT CLUB
Shoot: first Sunday each month
Rendezvous: September
Kenneth H. Lavery
5069 Gasport Road
Gasport, NY 14067

ELBRIDGE ROD & GUN CLUB
Shoot: October
Jim Peek
1541 Elm Street Ext., RD-2
Groton, NY 13073

FORT TICONDEROGA M.L. ASSOCIATION
Shoot: September
Jackie Trombley
9 Holcomb Avenue
Ticonderoga, NY. 12883

LAND OF THE SENECAS M.L. CLUB
Turkey shoot: November
Frank "Zeb" Zemanek
P.O. Box 476
Mreesport, NY 14816

LONG ISLAND B.P. RIFLES
Silhouette shoot: September
Turkey shoot: November
Blanket shoot: December
William E. Meess
P.O. Box 162
Seaford, NY 11783

OLD SARATOGA M.L. CLUB, INC.
Primitive Rendezvous: October
Joan Root
(518) 695-6415

THE RACOON LODGE
Shoot: second and fourth Sunday each month
409 Pleasantview Court
Copiague, NY 11726

NORTH CAROLINA

ALAMANCE LONG RIFLES
Fall shoot: October
Robert H. Fonville
1308 West Davis Street
Burlington, NC 27215

CROSS CREEK LONGRIFLES
Shoot: third Saturday each month
Jim Maxson
1007 Cain Road
Fayetteville, NC 28303

FRONTIERSMEN M.L. GUN CLUB, INC.
Shoot: third Sunday each month
Chris Hord
(919) 851-0051

LA FAYETTE LONG RIFLES
Shoot: fourth weekend each month
Mary E. Bailey
Route 1, Box 316A
Faquay-Varina, NC 27526

OLD NORTH STATE FREE TRAPPERS
Fall shoot: October
Vickie Deal
Route 1, Box 428
Claremont, NC 28610

YADKIN VALLEY LONG RIFLES, INC.
Shoot: first Sunday of each month
Fall shoot: October
Ronny O. White
P.O. Box 911
Elkin, NC. 28621

NORTH DAKOTA

RENEGADE RIFLEMEN, INC.
Shoot: weekly on Wednesday nights May through
September
Rendezvous: May
Kerry Eggert
1338 SW 10th
Valley City, ND 58072

OHIO

BACKWOODMENS M.L. RIFLE CLUB
Shoot: fourth Sunday each month
Arthur Brown Jr.
Route 2, Box 81
Gallipolis, OH 45631

BALL & ARROW PRIMITIVE WEAPONS CLUB
Woods walk: September
Rendezvoua: January
Bob Gilmore
103 Rear West 21st
Dover, OH 44622

BILL MOOSE M.L. GUN CLUB
Ohio state shoot: September
Turkey shoot: November
Beef shoot: January
Pork shoot: February
Jo Ann Case
(614) 471-7516

BLACK SWAMP M.L. RIFLE CLUB
James Woodward
710 Cherry St.
Findlay, OH 45840

BLOOD BROTHERS PRIMITIVE
WEAPONS CLUB
Ted Patterson
7559 Dry Run Road
Kingston, OH 45644

BLUE JACKET LONG RIFLES
Shoot: fourth Sunday each month
Steve Skidmore
117 Lincoln Avenue
Bellefontaine, OH 43311

BUTLER COUNTY SPORTSMEN RIFLE
and PISTOL CLUB
Shoot: first Sunday each month
Charles P. Antal
379 Kenyon Drive
Hamilton, OH 45015

BUZZARDS HOLLOW M.L. GUN CLUB
Dan Toth
4976 Newark Road
Mt. Vernon, OH 43050

CANAL FULTON RAMROD CLUB
Grocery shoot: first and third Sunday each month
Ray Heitger
317 East 7th Street
Brewster, OH 44613

CEDAR CITY M.L. CLUB
Grocery shoot: September
Turkey shoot: November
Grocery shoot: December
Richard Hoff
829 Danny Drive
Cincinnati, OH 45245

CINCINNATI M.L. RIFLE CLUB
Picnic shoot: September
TBA shoot: October
Turkey shoot: November
Grocery shoot: December
Bill Disbro
(513) 353-2955

COLUMBUS M.L. GUN CLUB
Mark Donaldson
(614) 272-1646

DAYTON MUZZLELOADING GUN CLUB
Shoot: first Sunday each month
David Merrelli
3346 Fair Oaks Drive
Xenia, OH 45385

DEATHWIND LONGRIFLES
Paper and Novelty shoots:
third Sunday each month
Don Miller
1700 Horns Hill Road
Newark, OH 43055

DOG CREEK LONGRIFLES
Shoot: third Sunday each month
Larry Morrison
P.O. Box 15
Middle Point, OH 45863

FORT MCARTHUR L.R. CLUB, INC.
Squirrel shoot: September
Hunters shoot: October
Turkey shoot: November
Quail walk: November
Sausage shoot: December
Trap shoot: February
Novelty shoot: March
Groundhog shoot: April
Kitchen shoot: May
Annetta S. Holmes
16108 County Road 155
Kenton, OH 43326

GREAT MIAMI LONGRIFLES
Rendezvous: October
Meat shoot: November
Jerry Stewart
(513) 492-7776

GREAT TRAIL PATHFINDERS
Grocery shoot: second Sunday each month
Gerry Juwell
P.O. Box 552
Malvern, OH 44644

HAWKINS MUZZLE LOADERS
Blanket shoot: September
Trail walk: October
Turkey shoot: November
Gary Habig
(614) 484-1517

KILL'UM BUCK LONGRIFLES
Rendezvous: November
Sheryl Swartzentruber
5411 Wadsworth Road
Orrville, OH 44667

LEIPSIC FISHING-HUNTING ASSOCIATION
Shoot: fourth Sunday each month
Dan Harshman
Box 52
Vaughnsville, OH 45893

LITTLE MT. FREE TRAPPERS
Shoot: last Sunday each month
Ben Wilcox
155 Arlington Drive
Painesville, OH 44077

MANSFIELD M.L. RIFLE CLUB
Woods walk: September
Rendezvous: October
Turkey shoot: November
5631 Lower Leesville Road
Crestline, OH 44827

MASSIE'S CREEK M.L., INC.
Over-the-Log shoot: September
Thurman Baker
1455 St. John Road
Jamestown, OH 45445

NEW FRONTIERSMEN
Rendezvous: September
Buffalo shoot: October
Turkey shoot: November
Robert G. Stickler
1352 Barbara Lane
Mansfield, OH 44905

OHIO VALLEY M.L. GUN CLUB
Joe Merrelli
7034 Linworth Road
Columbus, OH 43235

P.A. REINHARD M.L.R. CLUB
Turkey shoot: November
John Schopfer
215 South Wood Street
Loudonville, OH 44842

RAMROD BUSTERS
Rendezvous: September
Dale Muda
(216) 381-3169

SAND CREEK FREE TRAPPERS
Fall rendezvous: October
Turkey shoot: December
Sheila Guy
3811 Root Avenue NE
Canton, OH 44705

SANDUSKY COUNTY HAWKEYES
Fall rendezvous: September
Heritage Days shoot: October
Snip Dible
4370 Napolean Road
Fremont, OH 43420

SHAWNEE LONG RIFLES
Meat shoot: September
Turkey shoot: November
Ed Broyles
(419) 394-2833

SIMON KENTON LONG RIFLES
Shoot: third Sunday each month
Ken Brackett
7376 Normandy Lane
Centerville, OH 45459

SONS OF LIBERTY P.M.L.C.
Sonny Christman
6259 Beaver Pike
Beaver, OH 45613

STUMPTOWN LONG RIFLE CLUB
Over-the-Log shoot: September
David McGraw
Box 554
Bethesda, OH 43719

TOLEDO MUZZLE LOADERS
Merchandise shoot: September
Pumpkin shoot: October
Turkey shoot: November
Michael A. Thompson
3802 Garrison Road
Toledo, OH 43613

TREATY LINE LONG RIFLES
Rendezvous: October
Turkey shoot: November
Gary Bott
7868 State Route 305
Garrettsville, OH 44231

WRIGHT-PATTERSON B.P. SHOTGUN CLUB
Shoot: second Sunday each month
(513) 429-4113

OKLAHOMA

BETWEEN TWO RIVERS M.L. CLUB
Fall rendezvous: November
Shannon White
Route 1, Box 107A
Miami, OK 74354

CHISHOLM TRAIL GUN CLUB
Shoot: second weekend each month
115 N.
El Reno, OK 73036

CROSS TIMBERS PRIMITIVE SOCIETY
Shoot: last Sunday each month
John C. Copeland II
(405) 598-2679

LONG RIFLES OF THE CANADIAN/OKLAHOMA
CITY GUN CLUB/B.P. DIVISION
Shoot: third Sunday each month
Charlene Gilmore
7900 144th Avenue NE
Newalla, OK 74857

OSAGE TERRITORY M.L., INC.
Stew shoot: October
Over-the-Log shoot: November
Mary E. Good
P.O. Box 966
Claremore, OK 74017

RED RIVER MUZZLE LOADERS
Shoot: first Sunday each month
Glenn Bryan
506 South Main
Altus, OK 73521

OREGON

FOREST HILLS B.P. BRIGADE
Shoot: third Saturday each month
Linda Miller
3877 SE Walnut Street
Hillsboro, OR 97123

TRI-COUNTY GUN CLUB -
BLACK POWDER DIVISION
Shoot: second Sunday each month
Roger T. McFall
Route 5, Box 92-M
Sherwood, OR 97140

PENNSYLVANIA

BLACK BOYS OF BLOODY RUN
Turkey shoot: November
Lois C. Stoner
RD 2, Box 615
Everett, PA 15537

BLUE MOUNTAIN MUZZLE LOADERS
Rendezvous: September
Turkey shoot: November
Barbara Zerbe
(215) 488-6863

CAPTAIN PHILLIPS RANGERS
Meat shoot: September and October
Turkey shoot: November
Donald Keagy
(814) 793-2675

DELTA-PEACH BOTTOM FISH & GAME
Shoot: second Sunday each month
James Badders
4905 Clermont Mill Road
Pylesville, MD 21132

FIRST FRONTIER MILTIA
Shoot: second Sunday each month
Ronald R. Green
RD 1, Box 1891
Palmerton, PA 18071

THE FREE TRAPPERS
Blanket shoot: September and October
Turkey shoot: November
Dennis W. Keefer
RD 2, Box 339
Watsontown, PA 17777

GROVE CITY MUZZLELOADERS
Meat shoot: first and third Tuesday each month
Rendezvous: September
Jack Roddy
RD 1, Box 247 A
Harrisville, PA 16038

INDEPENDENT MOUNTAIN MEN
OF PENNSYLVANIA
Turkey shoot: November
Larry Leathers
RD 4, Box 231
Valencia, PA 16059

JEFFERSON COUNTY LONGRIFLES
Shoot: third Sunday each month
John Lee
Box 116
Brookville, PA 15825

LOYALHANNA LONG RIFLE ASSOC.
Grocery shoot: October
Turkey shoot: November
Blanket shoot: January
Jack Diehl
P.O. Box 813
Latrobe, PA 15650

OLD WESTMORELAND RIFLES
Blanket shoot: October and November
Dave Hykes
(412) 372-6285

PENNSYLVANIA FEDERATION OF B.P. SHOOT-
ERS
State match September
Jim Fulmer
RD 1, Box 1352
Hamburg, PA. 19526

PLUM CRICK VALLEY LONGRIFLES
Shoot: first Sunday May, October, and November
Frederick Grove
Box 54
Home, PA 15747

SAMPLE'S BORDER RANGERS
Rendezvous: September
c/o Tony Bombara
930 7th Street
Verona, PA 15147

SHESHEQUIN BUCKSKINNERS
Shoot: second Sunday each month
Turkey shoot: November
Rendezvous: February
Freda Schodt
HC Box 245
Trout Run, PA 17771

STANDING STONE MUZZLE LOADERS
Blanket shoot: September
Turkey shoot: November
James Leister
404 Orange Street
Mifflintown, PA 17059

SUSQUEHANNA POWDER HORNS, INC.
Shoot: fourth Sunday each month
Marie Rohleder
(717) 854-7251

TUCHAHOE VALLEY MILITIA
Hide and critter shoot: September
Turkey shoot: November
Don Blazier
331 Main Street
Bellwood, PA 16617

UPPER ALLEGANY MUZZLELOADERS
Shoot: first Sunday each month
Les Davidson
RD 1, Box 4
Pittsfield, PA 16340

WASHINGTON CO. BUCKSKINNERS
Blanket shoot: second Sunday each month
Bill Grego
711 Cummins Avenue, Apt. 8
Houston, PA 15342

WHISPERING PINES CAP & FLINT CLUB
Shoot: third Sunday each month
Paul "Skip" Hamaker
(215) 373-4419

SOUTH CAROLINA

BLUE RIDGE MOUNTAIN MEN
Shoot: last Sunday each month
Dave Schultz
(803) 296-3747

CAROLINA PO BOYS M.L.
Shoot: second Sunday each month
Jerome Wilson
Allendale, SC 29810

CHARLES TOWNE LONG RIFLES
Shoot: last Sunday each month
John Chapman
Route 2, Box 334
Moncks Corner, SC 29461

PIEDMONT MUZZLELOADERS, INC.
Shoot: third Sunday each month
Silhouette shoot: September
G.T. MacDonald
112 Mustang Circle
Simpsonville, SC 29681

ROCK HOUSE MUZZLELOADERS
Shoot: first Sunday each month
Greg Lutz
149 Effie Drive
Greenwood, SC. 29649

WACCAMAW MUZZLELOADERS
Shoot: Sunday following second Thursday each
month
Virginia S. Pruitt
722 A Juniper Drive
Surfside Beach, SC 29575

SOUTH DAKOTA

BROOKINGS RENEGADE M.L.
Frozen Foot Rendezvous: December
Terrence Hall
Route 2, Box 62
Bruce, SD 57220

HIGH PLAINS FREE TRAPPERS
Shoot: second Sunday April to October
P.O. Box 7794
Rapid City, SD 57709

CHICKASAW BLUFFS M.L.
Shoot: first Sunday each month
John T. Cleveland
6042 Tall Willow Drive
Memphis, TN 38115

TENNESSEE

CHUCKY JACK LONGRIFLES
Shoot: last Sunday each month
Fred Drumheller
5006 Cloverdale Ln.
Knoxville, TN 37918

DAVY CROCKETT LONG HUNTERS
Shoot: last Sunday each month
Jeffery E. Johnson
(615) 762-1415

ELK RIVER LONG RIFLES
Shoot: second Saturday each month
John Anderson
900 Bragg Circle
Tullahoma, TN 37388

OWL HOLLOW GUN CLUB
Shoot: second Saturday March to October
Sandra L. Fox
3013 Ironwood Drive
Nashville, TN 37214

TRI-COUNTY MUZZLE LOADERS
Shoot: third Sunday each month
Pat Nash
P.O. Box 402
White House, TN 37188

TEXAS

ALAMO M.L. GUN CLUB
Shoot: third Sunday each month
Alex Hamilton
1449 Blur Crest Lane
San Antonio, TX 78232

AURORA B.P. CLUB
Shoot: third Sunday each month
Fall rendezvous: October
Peggy Keiper
P.O. Box 1473
Boyd, TX 76023

CHEROKEE COUNTY M.L.
Shoot: second Saturday each even numbered
month
Melinda Peevy
Route 8, Box 122
Jacksonville, TX 75766

COMANCHE PEAK M.L.
Shoot: second Sunday each month
Fall rendezvous: October
Gayle Paul
P.O. Box 24699
Fort Worth, TX 76124

DALLAS M.L. GUN CLUB
Shoot: second Sunday each month
Rendezvous: Jan.
Jerry Williams
308 Hilltop Court
Mesquite, TX 75149

GREENWOOD LONGRIFLES
Shoot: third Sunday each month
Ed Kana
318 Juniper
Lake Jackson, TX 77566

HOWARD COUNTY MUZZLELOADERS
Shoot: first Sunday each month
Lou Key
1210 Lloyd Street
Big Spring, TX 79721

INDIAN RUN MUZZLE LOADERS
Shoot: second Sunday each month
Rick Scott
Box 1048
Big Spring, TX 79721

PASADENA M.L.
Shoot: fourth Sunday each month
Denise Yates
36 North Erik Drive
Angelton, TX 77515

PESO PRIMITIVE SHOOTERS
Shoot: third Sunday each month
Samuel L. Witt
509 Irondale
El Paso, TX 79912

THE POWDER HORN CLUB
Shoot: second Sunday each month
Mary C. McGill
P.O. Box 98
Southmayd, TX 76268

RANGER SPRINGS SKINNERS
Shoot: first Sunday each month
Fred Storing
1043 Westwood
Lewisville, TX 75067

RED RIVER RENEGADES
Shoot: last Sunday each month
Turkey shoot: October
Paul Gwynn
1204 Cheryl Drive
Burkburnett, TX 76354

SAM HOUSTON M.L.
Shoot: third Sunday each month
Joe Lightsey
(713) 820-2383

TEXAS BUCKSKINNERS ASSOCIATION
Shoot: third Sunday each month
W. Bill Alexander
Route 4, Box 508
7814 W. Blair
Odessa, TX 79764

TEXAS M.L. RIFLES ASSOCIATION
Fall shoot: October
Frost on the cactus shoot: February
Denise Yates
36 North Erik Drive
Angelton, TX 77515

TEXAS PIONEER M.L.
Shoot: last Sunday each month
Winter rendezvous: January
Vickie Overpeck
6801 Sandra Lane
Corpus Christi, TX 78414

TRAVIS VOLUNTEER M.L.
Shoot: second Saturday and last
Sunday each month
Norman W. Williams
P.O. Box 116
Bastrop, TX 78602

UTAH

FREE MOUNTAIN TRAPPERS
Shoot: second Saturday each month
Marlene Clark
2009 West Celia Way
Layton, UT 84041

OGDEN VALLEY MUZZLERS
Shoot: second Saturday each month
Mary Wheelwright
276 East 4675 South
Ogden, UT 84405

MOUNTAIN MEN OF THE WASATCH
Shoot: second Sunday and third
Saturday each month
Turkey shoot: November
Karen Fischer
(801) 968-5275

ROCKY MOUNTAIN FUR CO.
Shoot: first weekend in August
Jerry Farringer
9502 Buttonwood
Sandy, UT 84092

T-N-T MUZZLELOADERS
Shoot: third Sat each month
Rendezvous: August
Leanora Mann
257 South 400 West
Lindon, UT 84042

VERMONT

ETHAN ALLEN LONG RIFLES
Blanket shoot: September
Cecilia Telefus
RD 2, Box 2503
Vergennes, VT 05491

VIRGINIA

APPALACHIA PRIMITIVE MEN
Monthly shoot:
G.W. Bush
1010 Summit Lane NW
Roanoke, VA 24017

BLACK CREEK LONG RIFLES
Shoot: first Sunday each month
Kay C. Young
Route 4, Box 189
Mechanicsville, VA 23111

BULL RUN MUZZLELOADERS
Shoot: third Sunday each month
Jack Schildt
7572 Remington Road
Manassas, VA 22110

CHESAPEAKE BAY FUR CO.
Shoot: third Saturday each month
Mark Buttles
(804) 599-9104

JAMES RIVER B.P. CLUB
Shoot: second Saturday each month
Raymond Johnson
(804) 526-5795

OLDE VIRGINIA PRIMITIVE RIFLEMEN
Shoot: third Sunday each month
Fall rendezvous: October
Gary H. Brett
507 East Vance
Murfreesboro, NC 27855

THE RIFLEMEN OF WYNNE'S FALL
Meat shoot: October
Dave Clark
214 Baily Place
Danville, VA 24540

SHOOTING CREEK MOUNTAIN MEN
Shoot: second Sunday each month
Paul H. Stanaland
P.O. Box 203
Rocky Mount, VA 24151

WILDERNESS ROAD MUZZLELOADERS
Shoot: second Sunday each month
Jim Hartlage
485 Lakeview Drive
Wytheville, VA 24382

WITTEN FORT L.R. CLUB
Shoot: second Saturday each month
Wayne Craig
Box 113
Richlands, VA 24641

WASHINGTON

BEAR CREEK MUZZLELOADERS
Shoot: monthly
Jim Eckard
4739 191st Place SE
Issaquah, WA 98027

CARIBOO TRAIL MUZZLE LOADERS
Shoot: first Sunday each month
Ruth Lester
P.O. Box 24
Ephrata, WA 98851

CASCADE MOUNTAIN MEN
Shoot: third Sunday each month
25825 104th Avenue SE, Suite 301
Kent, WA 98031

GREEN RIVER MOUNTAINEERS
Shoot: first Saturday each month
Rendezvous: Labor Day Weekend
Bill Green
23007 126th Street SE
Buckley, WA 98321

INTERLAKE MOUNTAIN MEN
Shoot: third Saturday each month
Rendezvous: August
Robert Ace
11848 104th Avenue NE
Kirkland, WA 98034

PENINSULA LONG RIFLES
Shoot: fourth Sunday each month
Roy Morgan
1223 East 5th
Port Angeles, WA 98362

SPOKANE FALLS MUZZLE LOADERS
Shoot: second Sunday each month
Jack Dolan
Medical Lake, WA 99022

TSILLAN VALLEY BUCKSKINNERS
Charles Leffler
1562 Wapato Lake Road
P.O. Box 342
Manson, WA 98831

WASHINGTON STATE
MUZZLELOADERS ASSOCIATION
D.M. Dolliver
P.O. Box 132
Bellevue, WA 98009

WEST VIRGINIA

BARBOUR COUNTY .36er's M.L. CLUB
Shoot: monthly
Lloyd Warren Stout
(304) 457-2476

MASON COUNTY LONGRIFLES
Shoot: first and third Sunday each month
Charles "Buck" Yonker
Route 1, Box 14
New Haven, WV 25253

MINERAL COUNTY & WESTERN MARYLAND
M.L. ASSOCIATION
Shoot: third Sunday each month
Fred Krieger
13807 Brant Avenue
Cresaptown, MD 21502

MOUNTAINEER FLINTLOCK RIFLES INC.
Shoot: second Saturday each month
WV flintlock championship: September
Gene Hyre
843 Hughs Drive
St. Albans, WV 25177

OHIO VALLEY MOUNTAIN MEN INC.
Shoot: third Sunday each month
Blanket shoot: September
James Petit
RD 4, Box 406
Cameron, WV 26033

POTOMAC VALLEY M.L. ASSOCIATION
Shoot: second Sunday each month
William L. Blankenbecker
P.O. Box 1165
Petersburg, WV 26847

WISCONSIN

CROSS PLAINS M.L. LTD.
Shoot: last Sunday each month
Thomas Serafini
(608) 274-3538

FORT OLD ABE MUZZLE LOADERS
Gregg Condon
(715) 834-3911

FORT ONEIDA MUZZLE LOADERS
Shoot: second Sunday each month
David Short
1945 County Road Y
Seymour, WI 54165

FOX VALLEY MUZZLE LOADERS
Fall rendezvous: October
Gary Hoewisch
Route 1, Box 905
Fremont, WI 54940

RIB. MOUTAIN. M.L. INC.
Shoot: first Sunday each month
LaVerne Prichard
3305 South Mountain Road
Wausau, WI 54401

RED RIVER MUZZLELOADER
Sandy Soquet
Route 2, Box 62
Luxemburg, WI 54217

SMOKEY HOLLOW M.L.
Shoot: first Sunday each month
Daniel Franklin
W142 N6746 Washington Avenue
Menomonee Falls, WI 53051

TAYCHOPERA M.L. INC.
Shoot: second Sunday each month
Mike Mitchell
5075 C.T.H. "TT"
Cottage Grove, WI 53527

WILDERNESS MUZZLE LOADERS
Meat shoot: first Sunday each month
Rendezvous: September
Mike Bacovsky
1701 Circle Court
Waukegan, IL 60085

WISCONSIN MUZZLE LOADING ASSOCIATION, INC.
Nick Bodven Jr.
16129 50th Road
Franksville, WI 53126

WYOMING

BEAR RIVER MOUNTAIN MEN CLUB
Rendezvous: August
William W. Smith
64 Donner
Evanston, WY 82930

BIGHORN BASIN M.L. CLUB
Shoot: first Sunday each month
Patty Tyrrell
Box 92
Shell, WY 82441

THE CROW CREEK FUR CO.
Shoot: third Sunday each month
Monty Branson
1706 Silver Spur Road
Cheyenne, WY 82009

DEER CREEK MUZZLE LOADERS
Shoot: first Sunday each month
Kathy Korn
P.O. Box 1402
Glenrock, WY 82637

FT. BRIDGER RENDEZVOUS ASSOCIATION
Rendezvous: August
Roger Kimes
(307) 787-3340

LARAMIE RIVER B.P. BRIGADE
Shoot: third Sunday each month
Dave Wilson
P.O. Box 1566
Laramie,WY 82070

PLATTE VALLEY MUZZLE LOADERS
Shoot: third Sunday each month
Bob Eveland
4845 North Antelope Drive
Bar Nunn, WY 82601

SPIRIT MOUNTAIN LONG RIFLES
Shoot: second Sunday each month
Charles Stickney
P.O. Box 532

Cody, WY 82414
WHISKEY MOUNTAIN BUCKSKINNERS
Shoot: second Sunday each month
P.O. Box 563
Dubois, WY 82513

WIND RIVER MUZZLE LOADERS
Shoot: second Sunday each month
Mike Cash
154 Marlatt Road
Shoshoni, WY 82649

CANADA

TRAILS END MUZZLELOADERS
Elaine Arnold
Rural Route 1
Chatham, Ontario
Canada N7M 5J1

APPENDIX C
BLACK-POWDER REGULATIONS

The following state-by-state list tells whether or not there is a special black-powder hunting season, what the minimum bore size is, and whom to contact for more information.

ALABAMA
No special season for black-powder weapons
Minimum bore: .40 caliber

For more information, contact:
Alabama Department of Conservation
& Natural Resources
64 Northern Union Street
Montgomery, AL 36130

ALASKA
No special season for black-powder weapons
No minimum bore

For more information, contact:
Alaska Department of Fish & Game
P.O. Box 3-2000
Juneau, AK 99802

ARIZONA
Special black-powder hunt (deer, elk, antelope)

For more information, contact:
Arizona Game & Fish Department
2222 West Greenway Road
Phoenix, AZ 85023

ARKANSAS
Special black-powder season
Minimum bore: .45 caliber

For more information, contact:
Arkansas Game & Fish Commission
No. 2 Natural Resources Drive
Little Rock, AR 72205

CALIFORNIA
Special black-powder season
Minimum bore:.40 caliber

For more information, contact:
California Department of Fish & Game
1416 Ninth Street
Sacramento, CA 95814

CONNECTICUT
Special black-powder season
Minimum bore: .45 caliber (patched round ball)

For more information, contact:
Connecticut Department of
Environmental Protection
165 Capitol Avenue
Hartford, CT 06106

COLORADO
Special black-powder deer hunt
Minimum bore: .40 caliber deer; .50 caliber elk

For more information, contact:
Colorado Division of Wildlife
6060 Broadway
Denver, CO 80216

DELAWARE
Special black-powder season
Minimum bore: .42 caliber

For more information, contact:
Delaware Division of Fish and Wildlife
Edward Tatnall Building
P.O. Box 1401
Dover, DE 19901

FLORIDA
Primitive weapons hunt for deer
Minimum bore: .40 caliber

For more information, contact:
Florida Game & Fresh Water Fish Commission
620 South Meridian Street
Tallahassee, FL 32304

GEORGIA
Special black-powder hunt
Minimum bore: .44 caliber

For more information, contact:
Georgia Department of Natural Resources, Game
& Fish Division
270 Washington St. SW
Atlanta, GA 30334

IDAHO
Special black-powder season
Minimum bore: .40 caliber deer; .50 caliber elk

For more information, contact:
Idaho Department of Fish & Game
P.O. Box 25
Boise, ID 83707

ILLINOIS
No special black-powder season
Minimum bore: .45 caliber

For more information, contact:
Illinois Department of Conservation
524 South Second Street
Springfield, IL 67206

INDIANA
No special black-powder season
Minimum bore: .44 caliber

For more information, contact:
Indiana Department of Natural Resources
State Office Building
Room 607
Indianapolis, IN 46204

IOWA
Special black-powder season
Minimum bore: .44 caliber

For more information, contact:
Iowa Conservation Commission
Wallace State Office Building
Des Moines, IA 50319

KANSAS
No special black-powder season
Minimum bore: .40 caliber

For more information, contact:
Kansas Fish & Game Commission
Route 2, Box 54 A
Pratt, KS 67124

KENTUCKY
Special muzzleloading season
Minimum bore: .38 caliber

For more information, contact:
Kentucky Department of Fish and
Wildlife Resources
592 East Main
Frankfort, KY 40601

LOUISIANA
Special black-powder season
Minimum bore: .44 caliber

For more information, contact:
Louisiana Department of Wildlife & Fisheries
P.O. Box 15570
Baton Rouge, LA 70895

MAINE
No special black-powder season
Minimum bore: .44 caliber

For more information, contact:
Maine Department. of Inland Fisheries & Wildlife
284 State Street
Augusta, ME 04333

MARYLAND
Special black-powder season
Minimum bore: .40 caliber

For more information, contact:
Maryland Wildlife Administration
Tawes State Office Building.
Annapolis, MD 21401

MASSACHUSETTS
Special black-powder season
Minimum bore: .44 caliber

For more information, contact:
Massachusetts Division of Fisheries & Wildlife
100 Cambridge Street
Boston, MA 02202

MICHIGAN
Special black-powder season
Minimum bore: .44 caliber

For more information, contact:
Michigan Department of Natural Resources
Lansing, MI 48909

MINNESOTA
Special black-powder season
Minimum bore: .40 caliber (rifled);
.45 caliber (smoothbore)

For more information, contact:
Minnesota Department of Natural Resources
500 Lafayette Road
St. Paul, MN 55155

MISSISSIPPI
Special black-powder season
Minimum bore: .38 caliber

For more information, contact:
Mississippi Department of Wildlife Conservation
P.O. Box 451
Jackson, MS 39205

MISSOURI
Special black-powder season
Minimum bore: .40 caliber

For more information, contact:
Missouri Department of Conservation
P.O. Box 180
Jefferson City, MO 65102

MONTANA
Special black-powder season
Minimum bore: .45 caliber

For more information, contact:
Montana Department of Fish & Game
120 East 6th St.
Helena, MT 59601

NEBRASKA
Special black-powder season
Minimum bore: .40 caliber

For more information, contact:
Nebraska Game & Parks Commission
P.O. Box 30370
Lincoln, NE 68503

NEVADA
Special black-powder season
Minimum bore: .44 caliber

For more information, contact:
Nevada Department of Wildlife
P.O. Box 10678
Reno, NV 89520

NEW HAMPSHIRE
Special black-powder season
Minimum bore: .40 caliber

For more information, contact:
New Hampshire Fish & Game
34 Bridge Street
Concord, NH 03301

NEW JERSEY
Special black-powder season
Minimum bore: .44 caliber

For more information, contact:
New Jersey Division of Fish, Game & Wildlife
CN 400
Trenton, NJ 08625

NEW MEXICO
Special black-powder hunt (deer, elk, antelope)
Minimum bore: .40 caliber

For more information, contact:
New Mexico Game & Fish Department
Villagra Building, State Capitol
Santa Fe, NM 87503

NEW YORK
Two special black-powder hunts
Minimum bore: .44 caliber

For more information, contact:
New York Department of E
nvironmental Conservation
Wildlife Resources Center
Delmar, NY 12054

NORTH CAROLINA
Special black-powder season
No minimum bore

For more information, contact:
North Dakota Wildlife Resources Commission
Archdale Building
512 N. Salisbury Street
Raleigh, NC 27611

NORTH DAKOTA
No special black-powder season
Minimum bore: .44 caliber deer; .50 caliber
bighorn sheep, elk, moose

For more information, contact:
North Dakota Game & Fish Department
2121 Lovett Avenue
Bismark, ND 58505

OHIO
Special black-powder season
Minimum bore: .38 caliber

For more information, contact:
Ohio Department of Natural Resources
Fountain Square
Columbus, OH 43224

OKLAHOMA
Special black-powder season
Minimum bore: .40 caliber

For more information, contact:
Oklahoma Department of Conservation
1801 N. Lincoln,
Box 53465
Oklahoma City, OK 73105

OREGON
Special black-powder season
Minimum bore: .40 caliber deer; .50 caliber elk

For more information, contact:
Oregon Department of Fish & Wildlife
506 SW. Mill Street
P.O. Box 3503
Portland, OR 97208

PENNSYLVANIA
Special black-powder season, flintlock only
Minimum bore: .44 caliber

For more information, contact:
Pennsylvania Game Commission
P.O. Box 1567
Harrisburg, PA 17105

RHODE ISLAND
Special black-powder season
Minimum bore: .40 caliber

For more information, contact:
Rhode Island Division of Wildlife
Government Center, Tower Hill Road
Wakefield, RI 02879

SOUTH CAROLINA
No special black-powder season
Minimum bore: .36 caliber

For more information, contact:
South Carolina Wildlife & Marine
Resources Department
P.O. Box 167

Columbia, SC 29202
SOUTH DAKOTA
No special black-powder season
Minimum bore: .44 caliber

For more information, contact:
South Dakota Department of Fish, Game, & Parks
Anderson Building
Pierre, SD 57501

TENNESSEE
Special black-powder season
Minimum bore: .40 caliber

For more information, contact:
Tennessee Wildlife Resources Agency
P.O. Box 40747
Nashville, TN 37204

TEXAS
No special black-powder season
No minimum bore

For more information, contact:
Texas Parks & Wildlife Department
4200 Smith School Road
Austin, TX 78744

UTAH
Special black-powder season
Minimum bore: .430 caliber

For more information, contact:
Utah Division of Wildlife Resources
1596 West North Temple
Salt Lake City, UT 84116

VERMONT
Special black-powder season
Minimum bore: .430 caliber

For more information, contact:
Vermont Fish & Game Department
Montpelier, VT 05602

VIRGINIA
Special black-powder season
Minimum bore: .45 caliber

For more information, contact:
Virginia Commission of Game & Inland Fisheries
4010 West Broad Street
Richmond, VA 23230

WASHINGTON
No special black-powder season
Minimum bore: .40 caliber

For more information, contact:
Washington Department of Game
600 Capitol Way
Olympia, WA 98504

WEST VIRGINIA
Special black-powder season
Minimum bore: .44 caliber

For more information, contact:
West Virginia Department of Natural Resources
1800 Washington SE
Charleston, WV 25305

WISCONSIN
No special black-powder season
Minimum bore: .40 caliber (rifled);
.45 caliber (smoothbore)

For more information, contact:
Wisconsin Bureau of Wildlife Management
Box 7921
Madison, WI 53707

WYOMING
Special black-powder season
Minimum bore: .40 caliber

For more information, contact:
Wyoming Game & Fish Department
Cheyenne, WY 82202

BIBLIOGRAPHY

Carson, Kit. *Kit Carson's Autobiography.* Edited by Milo M. Quaife, 1935. Lincoln: University of Nebraska Press, 1966.

Chittenden, Hiram Martin. *The American Fur Trade of the Far West.* Vols. 1 and 2. New York: Press of the Pioneers, Inc., 1935.

Gowans, Fred R. *Rocky Mountain Rendezvous: A History of the Fur Trade Rendezvous 1825-1840.* Provo, Utah: Brigham Young University Press, 1976.

Hacker, Rick. *The Muzzleloading Hunter.* Clinton, New Jersey: Winchester Press, 1981.

Hansen, Charles, Jr. *The Northwest Gun.* Lincoln: Nebraska State Historical Society, 1976.

Clyman, James. *James Clyman, Frontiersman, 1792-1881.* Edited by Charles L. Camp. Portland, Oregon: Champoeg Press, 1960.

Mails, Thomas E. *Dog Soldiers, Bear Men and Buffalo Women.* New York: Prentice Hall, 1973.

Nonte, George C., Jr. *Black Powder Guide.* 2d ed. Hackensack, New Jersey: Stoeger Publishing Co., 1980.

Ross, Marvin C. *The West of Alfred Jacob Miller.* Norman: University of Oklahoma Press, 1951.

Ruxton, George F. *Mountain Men.* Denver: Old West Publishing Co., 1940.

Storm, Hyemeyohsts. *Seven Arrows.* New York: Ballantine Books, Inc., 1985.

Index

The Temple Gallery
6 Clarendon Cross, London W11 4AP
Tel: 071 727 3809 Fax: 071 727 1546

Robert Haber Ancient Art
16 West 23rd Street, New York NY 10010
Tel: 212 234 3656 Fax: 212 727 9669
and Artemis Group

EARLY CHRISTIAN & BYZANTINE ART

Textiles, Metalwork, Frescoes, Manuscripts, Jewellery, Steatites,
Stone Sculptures, Tiles, Pottery, Bronzes, Amulets, Coins and other
items from the fourth to the fourteenth centuries

Edited by Richard Temple

Texts by

Julius Asfalg, Barbara Deppert-Lippitz,
Hero Granger-Taylor, Jonathan Hope,
Natasha Kostotchkina, Andrew Spira,
Richard Temple, Marian Wenzel,
Klaus Wessel & John Anthony West

TEMPLE GALLERY   ELEMENT BOOKS

Also available from Element Books

Icons: A Sacred Art by Richard Temple

Icons and the Mystical Origins of Christianity by Richard Temple

First published in 1990 by
Element Books Ltd
Longmead, Shaftesbury, Dorset
in association with
The Temple Gallery
6 Clarendon Cross, London W11 4AP

© Richard Temple, 1990

ISBN 1 85230 214 3

Copy Editing: Gillian Bate
Design: Richard Foenander
Typesetting: Imprint, Oxford
Origination: Swan Litho, London
Printing: Javelin Litho, London